YOU MATTER

YOU MATTER

The Human Solution

DELIA SMITH

MENSCH PUBLISHING

Mensch Publishing
51 Northchurch Road, London N1 4EE, United Kingdom

First published in Great Britain 2022 Copyright © Delia Smith 2022

Edited by Karen Buchanan

Cover design by Philip Beresford. Front cover image © Greg Rakozy

Delia Smith has asserted her right under the Copyright, Designs and Patents Act, 1988, to
be identified as Author of this work

A catalogue record for this book is available from the British Library

ISBN: HB 978-1-912914-35-7; PB 978-1-912914-33-3;
EBOOK 978-1-912914-34-0

4 6 8 10 9 7 5

Typeset by Newgen KnowledgeWorks Pvt. Ltd., Chennai, India
Printed and bound in Great Britain by CPI Group (UK) Ltd, Croydon CR0 4YY

In memory of Etty Smith, who launched me
on this journey.

The challenge of conscious self-awareness is unlike anything that has occurred for millions of years. We are finding ourselves in the midst of a vast transition. How are we to respond? With respect to the universe itself, is there a reason for our existence? Is there a great work required of us?

Brian Swimme and Mary Evelyn Tucker,
Journey of the Universe

Contents

An Introduction

If you know me, or know of me, you might be thinking, 'What's going on here?' If you don't know me, let me explain: my former day job was an attempt to teach a generation the basics of cooking, via books and TV. Apart from a thriving website, that's now history, yet I have many unknown friends everywhere, and their warm responses and comments still give me a lift.

What, then, *is* going on here? It's something that's been on the back-burner for most of my life, with a long-held intention that it might one day become a book. Put another way, *You Matter* represents my burning desire to communicate something I'm now even more certain needs to be said, given the times we are living in.

It all began with me, aged about five, being put to bed too early. I knew it was too early because I could hear other children still out playing. So, wide awake, I began to think and reflect and daydream, quite naturally and contentedly, so much so that it became a routine thing. I was a bit of a tearaway and, much to my parents' great disappointment, not a success at school, but I always loved having time and space for quiet thought, and being sent to my room for doing something wrong was never the punishment it was intended to be. Fast forward through the years, always needing quiet time, and I now have a name for it: spirituality. Let me quickly say that it's nothing esoteric but, very simply, the result of an accidental prelude to a long life of reflective thought. What it involves is stillness, silence or quiet time. There are many ways of describing it, but in essence, it's having time and space in your life exclusively for yourself, to become more aware of a natural part of human existence that expands and invigorates your view of life.

After a lifetime of thought, I am now certain this is a crucial, yet much neglected, part of human nature. The presence of the human spirit, or the term 'spirituality', tends to be wrongly thought of as something otherworldly, and it is sometimes even made to seem that way. It can also be wrongly written off as something that is exclusive to religion. Mostly, though, this very natural spiritual dimension gets drowned out by surface life and its frantic overload. Yet with or without religion, when a natural dimension of human nature is not fully utilised it can leave a void, which sometimes leads to mental issues or inhibits the development of inner strengths we didn't know we had.

My thinking is that this vital, natural dimension in human life needs to be re-examined and revived. In neglecting the deeper aspects of life, we are missing out on what is probably *the* most important thing we should know: what an amazing thing it is to be a person and to be part of the collective human venture. This I now know with certainty, and it will be the central theme in all that follows.

Dissatisfaction with the status quo has increased since I started this project. The world and its precious consignment of life is in danger of becoming unhinged. There is no place to hide from the grave threat of climate change, as the deadly Covid-19 pandemic has reminded us. A wake-up call? Certainly, but in effect something far more – I see it as a call to arms. If things are not as they should be in our world, isn't now the time for a new human spirit to emerge? Shouldn't we engage in bigger, more ambitious thinking and become more aware of our roles as humans? We are at the helm, in control of how everything is to evolve and progress. We have to relearn how it's possible for our world to progress, while at the same time cooperating with nature in preserving our precious planet. How else can we ensure that our children's children, and beyond, have a future? If extinction is the unthinkable, well, it needs thinking about.

I have known or met some extremely talented people – some successful, some famous – who, in spite of their achievements, have not really known how good or talented they are; something blocks that *inside* knowledge and certainty of themselves. This also applies to humanity as a whole. The common malaise is that we *underestimate* ourselves and lack belief in our collective power and potential. As a result, the world is in chaos: we are decimating the planet that sustains and nurtures all forms of life. The deadly Covid-19 is, I repeat, not just a wake-up call, but a call to arms. After many years of reflection, I am certain that if enough of us buy into that call and are willing to explore the deeper inner dimensions in our own lives and the world, then a new dynamic spiritual energy can emerge. It is my firm belief that, in unity with one another, *human beings can achieve anything*. All the wars, factions and turmoil in the world come from not sensing this reality, yet that inherent sense exists in everyone, and can be found in silence, away from the noise, in the still, small voice of the human spirit.

I have divided what follows into what I call reflections, each with its own theme. They are meant to be read individually, perhaps over time, hopefully to encourage your own thinking. I have also included writings from great minds throughout the ages, as well as an eclectic collection of thoughts from all areas of life. What I had hoped to do, back when I was writing recipes, was to help and guide people through the basics, so they could eventually move on to more ambitious things. It's precisely the same here. There are far greater minds and writers on the following subjects, and I have included some suggestions for further reading at the end.

Spirituality is not confined to silence, but that silence permeates the whole of life and reveals new perspectives. We have much to learn and my hope is that you, like me, will discover that the challenge can be exhilarating. What follows is intended to be about you. Just as the universe is reflected in a flower, it is also reflected in you. My only goal in writing this is for you to know that you matter and are a unique part of this amazing human venture – what the biologist and conservationist Thomas Berry referred to as 'the greatest beauty in the known universe'.

Delia Smith, August 2021

Hope is like a path
in the countryside.
Originally there is
nothing – but as people
walk this way again and
again, *a path appears.*
Lu Xun

Who Was Pierre Teilhard de Chardin?

Pierre Teilhard de Chardin has inspired much of what follows. If, by way of introduction, I had to describe him in one word, it would be 'colossus'. He was a man whose thinking and vision was a century ahead of his time. He lived between 1881 and 1955 and was a Jesuit scientist specialising in palaeontology and biology. His work began with geological research, studying the origins of life found in fossils and rocks. This led him to what was to dominate his whole life and thought: the mysterious existence of life on earth and the supremacy of the human.

His insights were controversial, unacceptable to many scientists and theologians, and his church banned the publication of his essays and books during his lifetime. Yet after his death, his books began to be published around the world and people like Arnold Toynbee and Julian Huxley hailed him as the new Galileo. When HarperCollins, the publishers of his seminal work *The Human Phenomenon*, conducted a survey of the one hundred most important spiritual books published in the twentieth century, Teilhard's book was number one.

A book entitled *The Legacy of Pierre Teilhard de Chardin*, published in 2011, included a quote from Kofi Annan, former secretary general of the United Nations and a Nobel laureate, who in 2007 wrote about him, 'finally I am convinced that Teilhard de Chardin is a thinker for the twenty-first century'.

This is also my own view, and what follows here will hopefully introduce other thinkers to his challenging vision in these uncertain times. But first, some of his own words, taken from the preface of *The Human Phenomenon*:

> I doubt whether there is truly any more decisive moment for thinking beings than when, as the scales fall from our eyes, we discover that we are not an element lost in cosmic solitudes, but that within us a universal will to live converges. The human is not the static centre of the world as we thought for so long; but the axis and arrow of evolution, which is much more beautiful.

PART ONE

Rethinking Thinking

I

Exploding into Life

When you enter the Death Zone, the intensity is either overwhelming or extraordinary in its possibilities. I have no doubt that this pre-death period is the most important and the most fulfilling and most inspirational time of my life.

Philip Gould, *When I Die: Lessons From the Death Zone*

Strange, perhaps, to begin a book with death where the emphasis will be on the wonder of human life. In my own research, I have come to the conclusion that impending death can focus and sharpen the mind in a completely new energising, even fulfilling, way. A person who knows they are about to die can have a completely new perspective of their own life and the world around them. Hidden possibilities, resources and realities are suddenly revealed. It is almost as if a dying person can finally grasp the truth of what it means to be alive. This prompts a significant question: isn't it time to explore and uncover the deeper dynamics of human existence, *before* we reach the end of our lives?

Philip Gould's experience compelled him to write a book, in order to share what he called an 'intensity'. He wanted the world to know about it. There was obviously pain, fear and unimaginable suffering, but there was also something within human life that can enable a person at their very weakest to somehow completely rise above it, to know what is happening to them and find it exhilarating.

Years before this, back in 1986, I tore from a magazine a piece of writing that moved me very deeply; it is what initially inspired the title of this book. It was written by a young woman, dying of cancer, who wrote a book about her search for meaning, from the time of her diagnosis to her death.

Her name was Dorothea Lynch and the book was aptly titled *Exploding into Life*. Diagnosed at the age of thirty-four, she spent her remaining four years intensively searching to find meaning and purpose in her existence. Her co-author Eugene Richards described the book as 'a highly personal inquiry into what it means to be alive, to face the uncertain future and to accept death'. Big questions!

Even if you spent years researching the meaning and purpose of human life, it would be impossible to even attempt to synthesise the philosophies of the world's greatest thinkers. Yet this young woman, after four years of profound suffering while facing certain death, absolutely gets it. There is no mention of religion, but she knew, she saw what she believed to be the truth, and in just a few lines expressed it with astonishing certainty and clarity. I still find it impossible to read this without feeling deeply moved:

Mystery, what a mystery this life is. The plants are filling out. The garden out back of our home sprouts one half-inch here, one inch there, and I am changing, too; cancer plods on from node to node, remarkable and not remarkable at all, like summer itself. Just another growing season after all. Is this resignation? I hope not. I do not intend to give up without a struggle, but more and more I see myself as a thread in a huge and royal tapestry – important to the central design but having an end, a place, a physical destination. I think of the young daughter in Satyajit Ray's *Pather Panchali*, spinning, whirling in the rain, her hair flying out like a flag the night she died. No one is special, are they, when all is said and done? And, of course, each of us is very special, very singular, carrying weight. I matter. I would like to open the window tonight and yell that outside. I matter. Or go down and lie next to the plants and whisper it.

Difficult to find the words to follow that. It's simple, direct and conclusive, a piece of writing that needs some deep reflection. What is extraordinary is that she herself *wasn't* extraordinary. She was just an *ordinary* person like you and me, who, because of the situation she was in, took the trouble to try to figure things out. She understood that it was a mystery, but at the same time grasped with an assured certainty something of what belief is, and that human life is absolutely central to it. Her life, yours, mine – each one has a singular importance, but at the same time is part of a collective whole that has a place, an end and a physical destination.

Strong stuff. Not for cynics and scoffers, that's for sure. Yet there is a universal truth here that, in our current disconnected world, we somehow yearn to resolve. Dorothea's 'highly personal inquiry into what it means to be alive' is a challenge that anyone can take up. And why on Earth would we not want to? What *does* it mean? What is this amazing thing called human life in which we are all involved?

There are only two options in life, and both of them involve making a personal choice. One is to reject new ideas, be sceptical and take the line of least resistance. The other is to be open, to ask questions and to be willing to consider whether or not these questions may have answers. There is no middle ground: a refusal to make a decision is, in itself, a decision. As the American author Wayne Dyer put it: 'the biggest form of ignorance is when you reject something you know nothing about'.

Dorothea, given the circumstances she was in, felt compelled to search for understanding and meaning, and right there, in the midst of the darkest and most traumatic of circumstances, she discovered something within her own very fragile human existence, perhaps hidden before but now fully exposed: a powerful undercurrent of optimism and hope, which exists at the heart of all human life. And this is where any exploration into the meaning and purpose of the whole human adventure must begin and end.

2

What We Really Are

One may understand the cosmos, but never the ego; the self is more distant than any star ... We are all under the same mental calamity; we have all forgotten our names. We have all forgotten what we really are. All that we call common sense and rationality and practicality and positivism only means that for certain dead levels of our life we forget that we have forgotten. All that we call spirit and art and ecstasy only means that for one awful instant we remember that we forget.

G. K. Chesterton, *Orthodoxy*

'What we really are' is the central theme of this reflection, and the celebrated English author and philosopher G. K. Chesterton takes us straight to the point. As he asserts, we forget who we really are or, more starkly, we don't even know, because there are levels of life that get drowned out and are seemingly dead. Though they are not actually dead, because, as he points out, they are awakened when something moves us deeply and we remember. What

I think he means is that there's a massive underestimation within human life. We have untapped capacities we don't know about, buried beneath an outward show of control and rationality. I would depict it as a little flame in all of us waiting to be ignited and, at certain moments, when something bigger and beyond ourselves touches us deeply – art, music, poetry, the unexpected medal or winning goal – the flame leaps up and we are forcefully reminded of this hidden part of ourselves. We can call it 'goosebumps' or say that 'the hairs on the back the neck are standing up', but whatever we want to call it, something of beauty awakens in us and raises us above the daily grind to an awareness of the ecstatic. Chesterton also makes it personal, when he says, 'we have all forgotten our names'. And he so wants us, on that very personal level, to rethink and rediscover what we really are.

What's wrong, is that while we now know so much, we still know very little about ourselves, and particularly about the subtle workings of the ego that makes us fearful of the mysterious or the unknown, so the safety of our imagined rationality – common sense and all the rest – puts us in control. Thankfully, the true wonder of what we are can't always be controlled: the flame pops up from time to time, reminding us how human life is programmed and that it's perfectly natural to encounter deep moments of awe and intensity and 'all that we call spirit, art and ecstasy', because it's how we're made.

This is why adolescents, young people and older people wanting to experience all that life has to offer are sometimes vulnerable to distortions of this reality, which lead them to addiction to drugs, pornography, gambling, alcoholism or even to join terrorist groups. Isn't this a cry for help? 'Please give me some of the excitement, the energy and passion inside of me longs for?'

We can see a perfect illustration of this in the diary of Anne Frank. Pacing up and down within the confined space where her family were hiding and seeing the sun, the deep blue sky and the breeze outside, she wrote: 'I feel that it is spring within me; I feel that spring is awakening. I feel it in my whole body and soul.'

Another, much darker, illustration comes from the novel *Trainspotting* by Irvine Welsh. A group of spirited young men are also confined; this time by the circumstances of their drab, gritty lives on a housing estate rife with petty crime and drugs. They, too, long for 'everything', to escape a future of oppressive boredom in the only world they know. But their natural desire to 'choose life' and experience more than they can see ahead sadly leads them into heroin addiction, which they discover is a deadly and pernicious distortion of what the answer to human longing is truly about.

So, what is it about? What are we, *really*? History shows that we are creatures with unlimited scope and potential, but, as Chesterton laments, we sometimes settle for less, less life instead of more life. This can simply be a choice, a drifting inertia that lacks belief and settles for less. Imagine a two-year-old lazing around and taking things as they come, rather than a normal toddler who's into everything: wanting everything, trying everything without fear and absolutely up for life's adventure. Children often have so much to teach us, as does the bold Oliver Twist – and the important bit – he *dared* to ask for more!

Wanting 'everything' means that it's okay to dream, to be ambitious and to want to change things; it's a natural part of our make-up and what should be driving us. It's certainly not about status, wealth, celebrity, possessions or shallow things that fade with time. It's about wanting to be what we are meant to be – human beings who are fully alive and want more life, without fear and worry, with every sense awakened and with no 'dead levels'. Surely now, more than ever, as we face such an uncertain future, it's time to take on the massive challenge of life on Earth, to learn more and know more about that 'self, more distant than any star'?

3

The Scale of Things

We've repeatedly underestimated not only the size of our cosmos, but also the power of the human mind to understand it.

Max Tegmark, *Our Mathematical Universe*

Just one sentence, but what a positive message for all of us living in the twenty-first century. Tegmark feels that sometimes we humans can be a bit head-in-the-sand, thinking that all we can see is all that exists. As scientists are unravelling more and more about the size and scale of our cosmos, there's so much more to see. So, if our heads *are* in the sand, perhaps it's because we feel the enormous advances in cosmology might well be beyond our understanding. Not so, Tegmark is saying, we just *underestimate ourselves*. That's the important point he wants to make, and it will be a recurring theme.

So, with that on board, it's humbling to begin by standing back and considering not who and what we are, but what makes it possible for us to exist. Through the staggering advances of science and space exploration, we are now able to see Earth from space. There's satellite technology, space photography and even space archaeology, which can calculate from outer space where former civilisations existed on Earth. We no longer just gaze up at the stars through earthbound telescopes; our cameras and technology are up there alongside them, not just observing existing stars, but sometimes even watching new ones being born – including, incredibly, those being born billions of light years away! While cosmologists are attempting to define the size of our universe, they are discovering that reality might go way beyond it and there may even be other parallel universes. That's too much for me to take on board, so I'll take one universe at a time!

According to Tegmark, cosmologists have only managed to map out about 1 per cent of the known universe. But they do know the extent of it, and 'big' is not a big enough word – it goes on and on, to infinity. And yes, getting our minds around the idea is hard – endless space, occupied by trillions of stars, planets, meteorites and galaxies, some of them billions of light years away.

The awesome thing is that among all that immensity, seemingly packed to the rafters with eerily empty planets, one very tiny planet turned out to be unlike all the rest. In size, it is apparently comparable to a grain of cosmic dust, yet it is actually the most amazing phenomenon. Its surface is covered in vast oceans, deserts and teeming vegetation, and it buzzes with bright lights, motorways, shopping malls, theatres and sports stadiums. And guess what? This tiny, fragile fragment of matter we call Earth turns out to be a key player within that vast collective of anonymous planets. Why? Because it's the only one that bears life, as far as we know.

So the massive – and, as yet unanswered – question is: how on Earth (quite literally!) is that possible? Scientifically, although we know how life has evolved, the actual origins of life have not yet been forthcoming – what enabled the very first living cell to make the amazing leap into existence is still unknown. But what *is* known is how it's possible for life to flourish and continue to exist on this tiny but very significant planet.

Thanks to a fortuitous planetary arrangement, the universe has provided the precise conditions needed for life. Earth is encircled by a special group of planets called a solar system, which is part of a much larger group known as a galaxy, and two more key players within that, the Sun and the Moon. Planet Earth is positioned at the exact distance from the Sun that provides light, warmth and energy. A fraction closer and we would be a scorched inferno; a fraction further away and we would be a frozen wasteland. The Moon, reflecting the Sun, affects the law of gravity that governs the oceans, the tides and our measurement of time and calendar months. This wondrous and ingenious planetary formation around Earth provides a maternal comfort zone that sustains the precise conditions needed to initiate the evolution of every form of life – culminating in what must be its finest and most noble achievement: *human* life.

From here on the ground, it's hard to comprehend the awesome scale of things, but I'm always fascinated to hear how astronauts react when they are able to look down at Earth from space. One of them, Edgar Mitchell, described how profoundly it changed him. Afterwards, he felt a greater sense of responsibility and wanted to try to make a difference, to make sure humanity didn't annihilate itself or get bogged down by petty human problems.

I heard another astronaut say that, as he gazed down at the Earth and saw it suspended in space, he felt moved by the sudden realisation of what human life is: a tiny child with a thirst for life, reaching out to touch things, wanting to open everything, explore everything, know about everything.

Can there be anyone who hasn't had a cosmic moment of wonder as they gaze up at the sky on a starry night and wonder how it is that we are connected to it all? A couple of years ago, I attended a lecture by the cosmologist Paul Shellard. He described the universe as 'a grand design of seamless potential' and said something that has always stayed with me: 'the only appropriate response to the reality of the cosmos is humility'.

The following piece from *The Brothers Karamazov* by Fyodor Dostoyevsky beautifully describes someone having an intense cosmic moment:

The vault of heaven, studded with softly shining stars, stretched wide and vast over him. From the zenith to the horizon, the Milky Way stretched its two arms dimly across the sky. The fresh, motionless, still night enfolded the Earth … The silence of the Earth seemed to merge into the silence of the heavens, the mystery of the Earth came in contact with the mystery of the stars… Alyosha stood, gazed, and suddenly he threw himself down flat upon the Earth.

He did not know why he was embracing it. He could not have explained to himself why he longed so irresistibly to kiss it, weeping, sobbing and drenching it with his tears, and vowed frenziedly to love it, to love it for ever and ever. What was he weeping over? Oh, he was weeping in his rapture even over those stars which were shining for him from the abyss of space, and he was not ashamed of that ecstasy.

4

Small Wonder

A fragment of matter formed of particularly stable atoms broke away from the surface of the sun, without cutting the ties attaching it to the rest of things and at just the right distance from the parent star to feel its radiation at moderate intensity ... One more star had just been born – this time, a planet, imprisoning the human future within its globe and motion ... Let us restrict our attention and concentrate on this minimal, obscure, but fascinating object that has just appeared ... Let us look at the juvenile Earth, balancing there in the depths of the past, so fresh and charged with nascent powers.

Teilhard de Chardin, *The Human Phenomenon*

The time was something like 4.5 billion years ago; the place, somewhere within the immensity of the universe. At a particular moment, something unimaginably significant happened: planet Earth, the world as we now know it, was being born. Yet this was not just one more planet added to the countless trillions; this mysterious newly born planet, 'charged with nascent powers', is, as Teilhard says, *different*.

From where we are now, the momentous event is extremely hard to contemplate. First of all, it's difficult to appreciate what our existence on planet Earth is all about. What exactly is that very familiar (yet, at the same time, rather opaque) concept we call 'nature'? What is the current within the *natural* universe that, on one seemingly insignificant planet, begins to initiate the very first stirrings of what will then begin to breathe, move and have being? How does that same mysterious yet imperceptible current continue to push forwards, an ever moving and expanding flow of life, so that something that exists gives birth to something else, and something better, as the flow of life on planet Earth, overcoming all trial and error, determinedly continues to progress and unfold?

Fast forward billions of years, and this natural but determining epic that we call evolution, which has propagated every form of earthly life, reaches a seminal moment. Because what evolved was not just better, but the culmination of all that has gone before. Yet this time, it would be far more significant and spectacular: what evolved was the very first moments of a completely different kind of life. Human life, silently and unceremoniously arrived on the universal stage. If all the stars could have clapped and cheered, they surely would have. The vast, evolving cosmos gained a centre, and tiny planet Earth achieved something which would have unprecedented and unlimited potential: the human future.

This time, it was not just material instinctive life, but instinct that extended into fully blown *reflective thinking*, the birth of the conscious human mind and the dawn of the age of reason. When material life gained a mind, so did the universe, a massive reality that needs a lot of thought. From that moment, the natural current of evolution, rather than blindly and randomly pushing ahead, was taken over by humans, in partnership with nature. What was previously the animal instinct for survival and the first stirrings of consciousness blossomed into fully blown reflective thought, able to reason, invent and create.

There was no longer a need for genetic physical aids to evolve for survival; human ingenuity could now figure out not just how to survive, but how to *expand* life on earth with creativity and ever-increasing knowledge. Human ingenuity didn't just invent the wheel; it worked out how to navigate the oceans, fly aeroplanes, launch space shuttles and walk on the Moon.

Humanity is at the helm of evolution and has been enabled to reach beyond mere survival and to advance life on Earth, to be responsible for it and discover what sustains, surrounds and lies beyond it. And although it's not quite there yet, it will eventually uncover the full extent of those nascent powers.

According to science, our planet is still young and humans are a very young species. This should give us great hope for the future and may help to explain that, while we've certainly come a very long way, our species has yet to come of age. Despite advancing so far, we have not yet found lasting solutions to conflicts and chaos. Without realising, we are becoming an increasingly dysfunctional society – many are unaware of the catastrophic problem of climate change, for instance, let alone how best to resolve it – and we don't yet fully recognise our powers and responsibilities.

We may be evolving painfully slowly, even imperceptibly, but there is always movement. And despite our unresolved dilemmas and apparent failures, there is something undeniably honourable at the heart of humanity. Countless lives in very ordinary everyday circumstances bear witness to this, as people quietly and determinedly refuse to give up on hope, while wanting to have a hand in making a difference. I remember chatting to a housekeeper who was cleaning the floor in an intensive care unit. She had worked in an office for several years but said that she had decided to do something to help those in most need; she loved the work and found it so much more satisfying. Having a hand in making a difference fulfils something in us – something deep down that's in our destiny.

The cultural historian Thomas Berry wrote: 'Teilhard was one of the first scientists to realise that the human and the universe are inseparable. The only universe we know about is the universe that brought forth the human. Teilhard understood this; he understood that the human story and the universe story identify with each other.'

As we continue to grope our way towards the possibilities of the future, this deep-down part of us will provide the eventual solution to everything – and yes, that is the right word, *everything*. It's actually very simple; we need look no further than directly at ourselves, while asking some questions. What exactly is this phenomenon called human life? How is it that this mysterious gift of existence we all share has emerged over billions of years within the mysterious immensity of the cosmos? And why?

There are really only two reactions to that question. One is blind indifference – writing off human life as some kind of insignificant cosmic accident – and the other an innate sense of wonder at the possibility of belonging to something that does indeed have a purpose *and* a future. We're left then with pessimism or optimism, and it's difficult to make the wrong choice.

Our puzzlement regarding our destiny is especially poignant since everything else in the universe seems to have a role. The primeval fireball had the work of bringing forth stable matter. The stars had the work of creating the elements. The same is true on Earth. Each species has a unique role to play for the larger community. The phytoplankton in the oceans fill the air with oxygen and thus enable every animal to breathe. This is their work: to fill each lung with nourishing breath.

But do we humans have such a role? With respect to the universe itself, is there a reason for our existence? Is there a great work required of us?

5

The Unknown Phenomenon

The human is the unknown.

Alexis Carrel

And the solution to all we can know.

Teilhard de Chardin

Two short but sweeping, statements with huge implications. Alexis Carrel was a French surgeon and biologist specialising in tissue grafting almost a century ago. His words, astonishingly, are still true today, as certain elements of human life remain unexplored. And it is this thought that makes the implications of the second sentence so challenging and inspiring.

Once more, we need to ask what human life actually is. And *why* is it? And why do these very pertinent questions get glossed over? Human existence is an extraordinary and unparalleled phenomenon. Yet after tens of thousands of years of existence, we remain a mystery to ourselves, with scientists and cosmologists scratching their heads, unable to answer these questions.

Perhaps some of the greatest scientific minds, of the past as well as the present, are so preoccupied with what surrounds us that our own presence within the cosmos gets consigned to the back-burner. Surely it's time to raise the bar and to be a bit bolder, not just in attempting to discover what the universe is, but *why* it is, why life exists within it and whether or not there's some kind of game plan? Perhaps those powerful telescopes could be metaphorically turned around now and then and focused on our own unique little planet, which has managed to give birth to and sustain the only known forms of life in our universe.

Of course, for some scientists, human life is about nothing at all. In the grand scheme of things, we're totally insignificant and irrelevant, they patronisingly inform us, their arms tightly folded. Our planet is a fluke, a cosmic accident, a chance happening about as likely as winning the lottery. One television science programme even showed someone buying a lottery ticket, just to make sure that we understood the analogy. And yes, of course we realise that our planet may well have originally been a chance happening – thanks for the explanation, but why stop there?

We continue to make advances in the human sciences, and we now know every detail of our molecular, genetic and biological make-up. CERN in Switzerland, the European Organisation for Nuclear Research, is an amazing monument to science. The largest particle physics laboratory in the world, it is where scientists from all over the world contribute to 'uncover what the universe is made of and how it works ... to advance the boundaries of human knowledge'. It is breathtakingly exciting, a fitting tribute to nothing other than, wait for it, *human* ingenuity. But for all that, we're still left asking the question: what are humans?

Spot the huge dichotomy in this: why is it that some of the very greatest scientists are underestimating their own *human* ingenuity and power? Why are they, in essence, writing off as insignificant the human mind and its intelligence, which is at the heart of their own awesome achievements?

Fortunately, in the field of knowledge there is always movement, and more and more not quite so intransigent scientists are quietly breaking new ground in attempting to develop a science of the mind. This goes beyond the biological and material elements and explores the whole sphere of the human mind, which the physicist Max Tegmark has described as 'the most complicated and awesome thing yet discovered in the universe'. If Teilhard is right that the human is the solution to all we can know – and all the signs are that he is – we are still evolving in the area of the mind and slowly, imperceptibly, the conscious mind is coming to the fore as we become a more cerebral race.

Could it be that our very young species is on the brink of evolving into adulthood and entering a much more advanced sphere of knowledge? If so, this could make the third millennium a very exciting and challenging time to be alive.

6

The Mysterious Gift of Existence

Every child is completely individual. They are who they are.
Infant school teacher

Just imagine, for a moment, a small room, with three people in it. Then, at a certain moment, there is a very significant gasp for breath followed by a loud yell, and from that moment on there are no longer three people in the room, but four. How incredible. A completely new life has come to be; a new person exists, filled with promise and potential. Anyone who is closely involved with the birth of a baby can't help being caught up in the wonder of it. A midwife who delivered countless babies over several years told me that every single one felt like a miracle. That's about the truth of it, and the miracle continues, as any parent will affirm, after closely observing how the tiny, fragile life begins to develop and grow into a person.

Sadly, miracles get obscured as we are caught up in the frantic overload of daily life. Somehow, we cease to be amazed at things. After all, there are millions of babies born every day: let's not get too fussed or sentimental. No, let's not – babies are all very natural and normal. But if we go a bit deeper and reflect on the sometimes obscured reality of what constitutes a single human life, it's then that the sheer wonder of it really kicks in.

Reflecting on it throws up so many questions. How is it, for example, that no human who has ever lived on this planet has quite the same face as anyone else? Similar, yes; of a type, maybe. But precisely the same? Never. Even identical twins are always in some way different. Then, as if that isn't awesome enough, the next thing is even more so. No two people ever have quite the same voice; again, there are similarities, but each voice belongs exclusively to just one person.

There's more. Think thumbprints, which have long defined us as individuals, and now science has invented retina scanning, which reveals that no two eyes are the same. Finally, the scientific discovery of DNA recently affirmed that every human life that has ever existed has been totally and definitively unique. I'm stumped for words here – 'awesome' and 'phenomenal' don't quite seem to cut it. Metaphorically I need to kneel and bow my head at such a marvel!

Add all that up and still it's only part of the story. We are, as the saying goes, far more than the sum of our parts. What is irrevocably wired into our brains, and our material and biological make-up, is again a conscious mind; that, too, is not like any other, and it's what ultimately defines each of us as a complete and unique person.

On the surface of things, it's quite obvious to see: everyone has their own distinct appearance and personality. Each of us is a fully conscious person with a singular mind. We start out as infants knowing who we are. What then happens is that we gradually become influenced by parents, authorities, advertisers, television, newspapers, trends and so on. The psychologist Abraham H. Maslow describes us as 'pawns moved by others … or being put in an invisible straitjacket'. Yet the mind, though seemingly thwarted, isn't. We make up our minds, change them or have a mind to do something. Maturity means escaping the external overload of influences and knowing our own minds with certainty.

We are singular, material, thinking beings, with intelligence, imagination and creativity; if we are to believe in anything at all, surely we have to believe in ourselves. However, that is something we're not yet very good at, either personally or en masse. Not believing in ourselves seems to be a common malaise, yet, crucially, if we could remedy that, we could undoubtedly change the world. Why is it that we all run for cover rather than face up to the truth of our own unique, wondrous existence?

Sometimes old sayings offer us the very simplest and wisest advice. When will we stop burying our heads in the sand and see the wood among the trees? Every human life – yours and mine – is part of a powerful and dynamic presence in the universe, and it would be no exaggeration to say that we are its crowning glory. Our track record is there for all to see; as each decade and century unfolds, so too does our unlimited ingenuity and potential. Whatever our faults as a species, we can't deny the sheer wonder of every life that enters this world.

So, if humans are still a young species and are continually evolving and maturing, perhaps it is possible that a transition towards a more grown-up perspective on the value of our existence is ahead of us.

7

Mind Inside Matter

We are living in a material world and I am a material girl.
                                                    Madonna

The phantom of the opera is there inside my mind.
                                            Sarah Brightman

Everything has an inside as well as an outside. A simple statement, and a useful one to hang on to when trying to decipher the complexities involved in what defines human life. It is illustrated by two popular songs: picture Madonna, strutting purposefully across the stage and emphatically declaring that 'We are living in a material world and I am a material girl' and Sarah Brightman explaining in dulcet tones that 'the phantom of the opera is there inside my mind'. There you pretty much have it, matter being the outside, tangible part of what we are and the mind being the part deep inside. All pretty obvious and, at a certain level, taken for granted. What is extraordinary, though, is that while these two elements of our existence are, clearly, utterly inseparable, they have long been the cause of much fierce division. In one corner you have the rather lofty, otherworldly element, where material stuff is perceived as somehow inferior. And, in the other corner, you have the emphatic materialists who shrug off the mind stuff in favour of what's called positivism, which places an emphasis on the physical and tangible (mind stuff being a bit too mysterious and challenging).

Where the gloves really come off is between science and philosophy – not to mention theology! – where matter versus mind is one of the most fundamental divides. Perhaps if we become more focused on ourselves as a *species*, we could adopt a more grown-up view, in that mind and matter are totally interdependent, with neither side ever being able to reach the ultimate truth of human life without the other. Even if the whole of cosmology, physics and the natural sciences can know all there is to know about every particle of matter in the universe, they will still only have half the human story. As Teilhard pointed out, 'physics is left with thought in its hands'. My hope is that physicists, philosophers, theologians, psychologists and cognitive neuroscientists will one day complete the human picture by cooperating and working with one another.

While there is an abundance of biological human data, the thinking element – reflective consciousness – is a vast realm of the mind that is not yet fully understood. Indeed, some people are so materially intransigent and prejudiced that they staunchly deny that consciousness actually exists. This would seem to infer that we are a race of zombies, but without our innate intuition and reflective minds, how would we be able to figure out that we *were* zombies? And why didn't evolution produce zombies in the first place and just draw a line under it?

One thing is certain: the human mind is woven into the fabric of matter, so if you're a human being (and not a zombie) you are a fully conscious person, and knowing that you are is the simplest of realities. Teilhard's inspiring thoughts on mind and matter are that both should 'mutually enliven each other'. He knows it's difficult to grasp, so he offers what he calls a blunt formula: 'To think, we must eat'. To put it another way, you can spend all day thinking and reflecting on what a glass of vintage claret tastes like, but only by actually experiencing the joy of the senses of colour, taste and smell can you savour its sheer exquisiteness. Similarly, to appreciate a great work of art, music or literature, all your senses need to be engaged, but it also has to touch something deep within you, inside your mind.

The physiological understanding of how the brain works and how it's integrated with the philosophical workings of the mind is something we don't yet fully understand. However, we can be sure that we each have both a body and a brain and, in that very significant evolutionary step from animality to human life, we were also gifted the wondrous add-on of a conscious mind.

8

Consciousness: The Central Mystery of Human Life?

One spring morning in Tucson, Arizona, in 1994, an unknown philosopher named David Chalmers got up to give a talk on consciousness, by which he meant the feeling of being inside your head, looking out – or, to use the kind of language that might give a neuroscientist an aneurysm, of having a soul. Though he didn't realise it at the time, the young Australian academic was about to ignite a war between philosophers and scientists, by drawing attention to a central mystery of human life – perhaps the *central mystery of human life – and revealing how embarrassingly far they were from solving it.*

Oliver Burkeman, *Guardian*, 21 January 2015

Brave me! Given that the war continues to rage in academic circles, who am I to even dare to mention the emotive word 'consciousness' and whether it could be *the* central mystery of human life? Well, here goes, because it is a vast and infinitely challenging subject for *all of us* – not just eminent philosophers and scientists – and, while they continue to battle over definitions of what it means to be human, with (or without) a conscious mind, there are other options in our search for understanding.

Maybe it's us, the workers at the coalface of everyday life, who will be the first to come up with the answers. Why not? After all, everyone, young or old, knows who they are and has a mind of their own – each of us is a *self*-conscious person, quite different from any other. What's more, as I have already said, we all know that we know that.

However, for anyone trying to define the complexities of the conscious reflective mind, the trickiest part is always going to be language. So, in order to escape all the scientific and philosophical rhetoric, I'll try to take a simpler route.

David Chalmers, who has spent a lifetime studying the subject, uses a one-word description – *fundamental* – which, even for a lay person like me, is pretty easy to grasp. So, throughout these pages, I'm opting for consciousness as being fundamentally at the core or *centre* of our existence. Interestingly, even without precise definitions, we have developed our own everyday expressions for communicating what's going on at our *centre*, and it's this word that somehow encapsulates all the rest.

Think how often the word 'heart' pops up all the time. It has to be the most common way of expressing what's happening at our centre; biologically, it's the central organ that sustains material life, but the word also ends up being the natural equivalent in terms of the mind. The word 'soul' is also very much aligned to heart, and the two words are often used together – 'heart and soul'.

The concept also applies to collectives: humanity has a soul, as does the universe. Decades like the 1980s can have a soul. Soul music has an inner depth, and if you are the 'life and soul of the party', you are radiating a kind of inner wellbeing. The soul also connects people in a special way. Sometimes friends see themselves as twin souls or soulmates. For me, one of the greatest lines in English literature was spoken by Cathy in Emily Bronte's *Wuthering Heights* about Heathcliff: 'He's more myself than I am. Whatever our souls are made of, his and mine are the same.'

It was a passionate outburst that described something very intense, but also a glimpse of a hidden reality, whereby all human souls or consciousnesses are somehow centrally connected. My late mother was incredibly drawn to young people and always interested and wanted to engage with them. When she died, we received many beautiful notes saying how they had felt somehow understood and inwardly connected to her. It was very humbling.

I have long held the belief that language should be the servant of communication and not the other way around, so I hope I can safely say that when we say heart, soul or centre, we all know exactly what we mean. The reality of a fundamental fully conscious reflective mind at the very (here we go again) 'heart' of our existence – and within the universe itself – is deeply profound and awesome.

As David J. Chalmers puts it in *The Conscious Mind*:

Consciousness is the biggest mystery. It may be the largest outstanding obstacle in our quest for a scientific understanding of the universe ... we are entirely in the dark about how consciousness fits into the natural order ... This puzzlement is not a cause for despair; rather it makes the problem of consciousness one of the most exciting intellectual challenges of our time.

9

Elusive Spirit

Spirit: The force or principle of life that animates. The body of living things.

Collins English Dictionary

No concept is more familiar to us than spiritual energy. And yet nothing remains more obscure to us scientifically.

Teilhard de Chardin

The human spirit is always going to be difficult to define adequately, but I think the dictionary definition is actually spot-on. Spirit and spiritual things are not always on the radar of human knowledge because, as Teilhard points out, they remain scientifically obscure. Perhaps the concept of spirit is so familiar – we live with it, we know it and it's part of what we are – that pinning it down is unnecessary. For Teilhard, the force of life is a cosmic spiritual energy that permeates everything that exists; it's an interior current of energy, which inspires the way we think, act and feel. It's sometimes in 'sleep mode', hidden away until something awakens it, but, at more *spirited* moments, it's switched on and ready for anything.

For me, spirit is what inspires passion and moves people, and it can be spontaneous. Being a free spirit means being willing to take a chance or a risk, even if it turns out to be wrong. I learned all about this that when I ran out onto a muddy football pitch, urging the crowd to support their team more loudly. My mistake was forgetting that the match was on television! To say it was followed by a furore is an understatement; nowadays we would say it 'went viral'; one sportswriter even suggested that I should appear before an FA disciplinary committee. Yet a wise person I met a few days later told me that being spontaneous, taking risks in order to inspire others, is sometimes necessary, even if it fails. I wrote his words on a scrap of paper that I still have now. And what then transpired, for the most part, was an about-turn – I received many messages of appreciation and encouragement that now (thanks to TV) I have gained masses of friends in other football clubs all over the country, who, because they absolutely understood where I was coming from, identified with my actions.

Spiritual energy is available to all of us. It is not individual or exclusive, but something universal and uniting that enlivens our collective effort and creativity. So much so, that without even thinking about it, we automatically refer to it. There are all kinds of permutations, from a 'universal spirit' and a 'spirit of the age' or 'of the Earth', a 'human spirit' and a 'team spirit' and – the very best example of all –even when we are separated from others, we can 'still be with them in spirit'. There's also plenty of evidence of the communal unifying spirit that surfaces in certain circumstances. One of the best examples was the 'wartime spirit', when, in a time of great fear and uncertainty, an amazing, unifying spirit and determination brought people closer together. I was four when the Second World War ended, but I was brought up in the aftermath and witnessed first-hand the nostalgia for that communal closeness that seemed to disappear once it had ended. Just before the war, Winston Churchill was questioned, after a broadcast, as to why he did not fully explain the gravity of the impending conflict to the people. His reply was that he wanted to give a more optimistic slant on things, to encourage people to discover a *spirit within themselves* that they may not know they had.

That is a profound observation and, right now, the challenge for us all is to rediscover that spirit, even though we are not living in a time of war. It was inspiring to see so many people leaping into action to support each other immediately after the first Covid-19 lockdown was announced. This unifying spirit still surfaces; in the midst of the most harrowing circumstances, there are countless stories of courage. My own grandfather was decorated for risking his life to save others in battle at Ypres during the First World War. More recently, during the terror attacks in Britain, there were many acts of bravery, as people instantly leapt into action to try to shield others – among them the Millwall football fan who was slashed and stabbed by the attackers eight times as he succeeded in blocking the doorway of a crowded restaurant to save the people inside. What moves me most is that these are ordinary people, leading ordinary lives, who in a flash become extraordinary. While the human spirit may never be absolutely defined, it can never be denied.

Another striking example occurred during a time of celebration, when London hosted the Olympics. A woman I heard on the radio noted that while travelling on the London

Underground, things were somehow different – there seemed
to be a heightened spirit of warmth and friendliness among
people. In her words, 'I felt I'd caught a glimpse of how life
should really be.' During the Games, there was a heightened
awareness of what happens when nations ignore what divides
them and become a global community of *shared* spirit and
endeavour. For athletes, years of strenuous toil and labour
culminate in an awesome spectacle of spiritual and material
energy, working in tandem: the meticulous concentration of
the mind, while the body is being pushed to its limits, and
the determination to reach the summit and win the prize.
There are mistakes, failures and disappointments, but also
a celebration of shared achievement. There's national pride,
certainly, but also a deep sense of awe and pride in watching
what can be achieved by human beings from whatever nation
they represent.

For me personally, another moving and memorable
example of this human determination to succeed against all
odds was on the television news. In Syria, a young, injured,
pregnant woman was pulled from the bombed rubble that
was once her home. On the way to the hospital, she began
to go into premature labour. The medical team, working
unbelievably in the midst of all the noise of bombing and
gunfire, managed to save her, but her newborn baby did
not respond, and so they just set to work, refusing to give
up, pummelling and massaging the pale little infant, trying
everything they could to coax it into life. After quite a long
time – and what had seemed such futile effort – who could
have dared hope? Then it happened; suddenly, amazingly,
the tiny baby gave a gasp and let out a yell.

Witness the human spirit. Alive and active, in the midst
of such horror. The bravery of the medics, working in such

dangerous circumstances, their refusal to give up. And alongside them, an unseen but equally brave young woman, at very great risk to her own life, filming so everyone could see such a precious moment, which shone so brightly in the devastating brutality of war.

There are countless stories like this one that should give us more than an inkling of what we are truly about and what we are capable of. At a time of such chaos and uncertainty in our world, it's obvious that things could and should be different. And while the mystifying yet familiar human spirit may never be scientifically defined, it remains wired in, fully alive and active.

10

Spirituality Unmasked

The Teilhardian revolution – it is nothing less – in so much of our thinking finds its truest and most significant expression in the whole field of what we refer to as 'spirituality'. There is a whole list of terms – 'the spiritual life', 'spiritual reading', a 'spiritual outlook' – which perpetuate the notion of something esoteric, private, exclusive, associated with a small group of practitioners, set apart from the generality of humanity … This is a falsification of the true position … spirit is the ultimate reality, a spiritual outlook is the only outlook; all life at the human level is spiritual life or it is, quite literally, meaningless.

Thomas Corbishley, *The Spirituality of Teilhard de Chardin*

If defining spirit proved challenging, spirituality is much simpler. The above quotation from the first paragraph of a book by Thomas Corbishley immediately makes short shrift of all the distortions and falsification associated with the word spirituality. What he wants us to be sure of is that *all* human life is spiritual. Everyone is a naturally spiritual person; it's not just a dimension of who we are, but part of the very life blood that flows through our veins. While the term spirituality has traditionally been associated with religion, it now encompasses far more than that and has even become quite fashionable. Sadly, within either a religious or a secular context, it can still end up as being something supposedly set apart from the everyday earthiness of existence.

So why the increased interest in spirituality? Perhaps it's because a decline in established religion has left a vacuum and a latent hunger for a deeper, more reflective perspective on things. Much more likely and significantly though, it's a sign of the times, in that human life is beginning to move towards a more spiritual, cerebral era. Now, thanks to the development of new technologies and with artificially intelligent robots heading our way, we are going to have more available time.

Because of this change, spirituality has to be rescued from being something that is somehow set apart from most of us, and the first thing to grasp is how basic and fundamental it is to all of us. We all have reflective moments – even small children sometimes get 'lost in thought' – but what isn't always recognised is that we *all* have a natural capacity for *more* reflection and deeper thinking. Life, which careers along on the surface of things, filled with frantic activity, can drown out this vitally important part of who we are; even when we're doing seemingly relaxing things like watching television, reading or doing crosswords, we are still being active.

Giving time and space in everyday life to be still, silent and initially just to daydream will allow this sometimes neglected, but natural, capacity to expand into something deeper, which can open up new perspectives on things. There's nothing grandiose or high-flown here – just a gentle unfolding of a more considered view of life.

One of the false interpretations attached to spirituality is that it somehow withdraws us from the affairs of the world, when in fact it does the opposite. When you consider the world and reflect on things, life begins to take on a sharper focus and becomes more vibrant and interesting.

One way to bring spirituality instantly down to earth would be to compare it to spending time at the gym or doing exercise. Neglected muscles become flabby, which induces a kind of lethargy that can restrict us physically, whereas with regular exercise, the whole body begins to wake up, becoming fitter and stronger. Likewise spending an equal amount of time being still and silent expands us spiritually, and precisely the same thing happens to our neglected inner self – it begins to awaken, develop and become stronger. This deeper thinking leads us to sense that there's more to life than we thought – that there are new horizons and possibilities. Our world expands and becomes more fascinating and interesting. Spending time on this much-neglected inside life enkindles in us what Teilhard describes as an increased 'zest for life', which enables us to experience what he calls 'more life'. If our enriching spiritual lives are left dormant, we may be only half alive and oblivious to life's ever-expanding experiences.

I seem to recall someone at the start of the twenty-first century predicting that this would be 'the thinking century'. Maybe with the decline of physical labour and an increase in leisure time, we will become more spiritually engaged and focused on learning. The positive side of all this extra time is that it will enable us to stand back and think through how we can best find solutions to the turmoil in our world. Are we all too busy to stop and reflect on how as a species – or, if you like, a *human family* – we can begin to find solutions and *collectively* work together to build a better future? While our world appears to be evolving at a very fast rate technologically, a much quieter but equally significant evolution is going on – the expansion of a collective consciousness that will have a bearing on our future.

In her book *The Search For Spirituality*, Ursula King has documented a wide-ranging account of the current interest in spirituality throughout the world. In the first edition, she quoted what is, for me, possibly the best, most lucid description of precisely what spiritual development is, which was taken from the 1994 Ofsted *Handbook for the Inspection of Schools*:

> Spiritual development relates to that aspect of *inner life* through which pupils acquire insights into their *personal* existence which are of enduring worth. It is characterised by *reflection*, the attribution of meaning, to experience, valuing a non-material dimension to life and intimations of *an enduring reality*. 'Spiritual' is not synonymous with 'religious'; all areas of the curriculum may contribute to a pupil's spiritual development.

All the italics are mine, and I would also add: 'not just all areas of the *curriculum* but all areas of *life*.'

The following is an extract from King's book:

> For the adult educator, the question is how to encourage the growth of the children's innate spiritual sense, how to expand their awareness, their deep sense of mystery,

their original trust in the ultimate goodness of the world and life. The story of a first-grade class is told where the teacher tried to still the noisy activity of small children at play by making them sit down on the floor, inviting them to look quietly at the light of a candle in the middle of the room – a focus for their vision and the gathering-in of their thoughts. The children liked that so much that, a week later, they eagerly asked: 'Please, when can we have that candle thing again?' They obviously enjoyed that beautiful moment of quiet, a space for coming to themselves in stillness, so precious yet so rare in a world of constant movement and activity.

II

A Personal Project

A real person is his or her own determinant ... every person, in part, is his or her own project and therefore makes his or her self ... and looks within for guidelines, values and rules to live by. A place for contemplation and for all other forms of going into the self, away from the outer world, helps people to become what they can and deeply need to become. The contemplation and the enjoyment of the inner life not only is a kind of 'action' in itself, it produces stillness, the cessation of muscular activity. The ability to wait to discover what it is like to discover, not to invent or construct, and teaches the ability to wait.

Abraham H. Maslow, *Motivation and Personality*

Looking 'within for guidelines, values and rules to live by ... helps people to become what they can and deeply need to become.' The dynamic of that short phrase more or less sums up everything that is written within these pages. Abraham H. Maslow was an outstanding psychologist and deemed by *Esquire* magazine one of the most influential people in the first half of the twentieth century. He conducted research into the depth and magnitude of the human mind that was absolutely ground-breaking. Instead of working in laboratories, studying data and dealing with the psychologically sick, he took the unprecedented step of asking the complete opposite question: why were some people psychologically healthy? He interviewed thousands of people and discovered that those without psychological disorders were self-determining, knew themselves and their own minds, and made their own decisions without outside pressures or influences. He called this being 'self-actualised' or 'self-fulfilled'.

I love this piece of writing because he is explicitly saying *how*. If a person has the *will* to act on their own behalf, to become their own project, be self-determining and discover their own hidden depths, it will inevitably involve finding a place for contemplation, going into the self, away from the outer world, enjoying an inner life, being still and discovering the ability to wait. It begins with a decision to *choose* to commit to a personal 'me' project, to become open to my own possibilities and potential, to discover what I don't yet know but *can* know.

Looking at the current state of the world, it's the psychologically dis-eased who are both most in need and most responsible for the turmoil – not through innate badness, but through ignorance of the nobility and goodness of human life that can only be perceived from knowing the inner depth of human nature.

All psychologists agree that we need space and reflection in our crowded lives, yet there is also an inexplicable resistance. Some people would rather walk to the ends of the earth than give themselves personal time and space. Maybe we have just got into the habit of being busy, although our resistance could also be due to historical reasons. In the nineteenth century, religion in the West was largely thrown out, along with the spiritual dimension of inner life, which was wrongly assumed to have been exclusive to religion. This was a momentous loss of a vital and necessary part of being human. Given that we have a huge capacity for something that is no longer there, its absence has left a deep void in people's lives, and a part of us now missing in the modern world. Perhaps this capacity for a natural spirituality is contributing to our over-activity as we attempt to fill the void, and suppressing something natural could be the cause of many mental health issues. Looking at the current problems in the world, we could hardly describe humanity as mentally healthy. Maslow dedicated his life to uncovering what he boldly called 'the greatness in each and every one of us'. The hidden depths of human nature, he thought, can be revealed to anyone who is willing to engage in a personal project of self-therapy.

Over a lifetime of research, Maslow became certain that every human life mattered. He also observed that knowledge of one's own nature is consistent with knowledge of human nature in general. Self-fulfilled people have a deep identification with and sympathy and affection for other human beings, and a genuine desire to help the human race.

Meanwhile, the world's turmoil demands that as many of us as possible engage in a personal spiritual project. It's free and only involves two things. One is a commitment. The second thing, and the really tricky bit – but only initially – is finding the time. Escaping from habitual overload is not easy, but requires intelligent reasoning. It is easy to spend half an hour on Facebook, reading a newspaper or watching a television show, but giving yourself space to be still and silent can somehow be a huge issue. Perhaps the reluctance is not about time at all, but an element of fear. Here, if I could give you a money-back guarantee, I would. There *is* nothing to fear. In fact, the opposite happens; self-therapy deals with fear and anxiety. If I had to use a single word to describe the effects of this, that one word would be *reassurance.* Peaceful silence calms fear, not only restoring tired limbs but quietening anxious minds. If you are willing to commit to it, you will soon stop being afraid and discover how to be tender with yourself and be open to new perspectives and possibilities that you had no idea of.

This often begins with reflective daydreaming, but someone who made a real commitment to it found that wasn't the case. Her random thoughts brought up some big issues in her life that had not been dealt with – things that get buried away sometimes need a conscious airing. Over time, practising self-therapy begins to reassure us, freeing us from our doubts and uncertainties; it teaches us not to be afraid to fail, and instead helps us realise that there is no condemnation coming from anywhere. There are reasons for everything, which are not always in our control. Faults and failings are universal and part of the human lot. There's no such thing as a perfect person, and just knowing that is a step towards freedom. On the outside, we have burdens laid upon us and are sometimes plagued by mistakes and anxieties, but on the inside we discover our own truth and values. Perhaps the greatest revelation of all is understanding that we have the resources to do that ourselves. As the fragile inner spiritual self grows stronger we find, in among life's pain and disappointments which all of us have to undergo, that there is also hope and inner joy. This is not in any way a withdrawal from outside life, but the opposite; it is an awareness of losing yourself in something greater than yourself and a stronger identification with the rest of humanity, a sense of belonging and wanting to play a part in its future.

There is nothing grandiose about this, and nothing *has* to be achieved. One of Maslow's brilliant expressions is that our disposition should be 'a healthy openness to the mysterious, and a realistically humble recognition that we don't know much', which keeps everything well-grounded. The antidote to chaos is 'to look within for guidelines, values and rules to live by'.

I was always passionate about understanding religion and spirituality and then, to cut a long story short, about twenty years ago, reflection became a much more serious commitment. I read about an Indian Sufi who said that if you want to be serious about understanding the spiritual life, it is absolutely necessary to spend a minimum of thirty minutes alone every day, in silence. I can't tell you how many books I had read before then, but no one had actually spelt it out and said how. He knew, as I do now, that in the current climate it was a big ask, so he suggested starting with ten minutes and then increasing it to twenty, but you *had* to end up with at least thirty minutes, but ideally one hour. I made the decision and commitment, and very soon found it was something I couldn't do without, ending up with an hour every day.

All this is a personal testimony, but a few practical points might be helpful. Choose your best time – whether you're a night person or a morning person. Try to ignore how you feel – it's the commitment that counts. A timer is useful initially, instead of constantly checking to see if the time is up. And relax – you don't have to be rigidly still, just not walking about. All you have to do is let your mind go where it will. Sometimes it leads into deeper thoughts, sometimes not – thinking what you might have for breakfast is okay. It's just about getting used to allowing yourself to be soothed by silence and not influenced by anything – except perhaps a short reading or one of the quotes in this book, which can provide a springboard for deeper thought. Remember: Rome wasn't built in a day, and the harder it is to be still, the more it is needed. What we are learning is the ability to wait.

There are, of course, many versions of the above that all fall under the generic umbrella of 'meditation'. This is not a word I would use, because for years I knew that I would never be able to meditate in the way that some people were teaching – I had no chance of emptying my teeming mind! Some of these ideas can also be rather high-flown, giving the impression that meditation somehow elevates people; not so. The fruits of everyday silence and tranquillity are humility and a greater empathy towards the world. Again, every person is his or her own project, and we can all learn from one another and hopefully experience the 'contemplation and the enjoyment of the inner life'. As Maslow says encouragingly: 'The world is latent inside you.'

12

The Examined Life

To know yourself is the beginning of wisdom. The unexamined life is not worth living.

Socrates

Socrates was one of the earliest great thinkers, and these much-quoted lines cleverly pose important questions. It was at a certain moment in history, in a designated place somewhere on this planet, that something amazing happened: as the Earth travelled on its 365-day orbit around the sun, on a specific day and at a precise moment in time, *you* came into this world. You were given a name and, from that moment, became a unique presence within the universe that was to be your home. You are part of something, and though you might have no idea *what*, deep inside, you might have a kind of inkling. And however obscure, fleeting or fragile that thought is, it connects you to all that exists.

The big question is always going to be: 'Why?' Why were you born into the world and the universe – and what is the meaning of the inescapable reality you now call your life? We have the most phenomenal means of seeking and finding the answers, as each of us has a conscious reflective mind – a virtual treasure trove of resources, imagination and creativity. So why would we not want to know ourselves and have a life that's worth living? It might seem difficult, but the thought that leads to knowing ourselves is actually, in essence, something passive.

Sometimes, works of art can speak far more loudly than words about the great truths of life. For me, the sculptor Auguste Rodin's masterpiece *The Thinker* powerfully illustrates the phenomenon of thought. The imposing human figure represents the powerful physicality that is expended in human endeavour, while the head resting on the hand portrays someone purposefully engaged in deep thought. It movingly depicts what we are, showing our material striving alongside the mind's central role in our existence.

Rodin's figure is not being clever, he's just content to sit still, be silent and *give himself time* for thought. It is so simple, so basic and, for those who *want* to see, it's all about choice. We all have choices, and I am the one who chooses what I want in my life.

Once again, knowing yourself has to involve spending precious time alone. If you want to get to know someone, you have to spend time with them. And *real* time – not in a crowd, but one to one. It's also the only way you can get to know either someone else or yourself. What do I really think about my life, the world and the universe? The worst-case scenario is indifference: not considering what's in my head or my heart, and so never experiencing that amazing human capacity for *more* life. Knowing yourself and being sure of your own inner value opens up new vistas, as egoism falls by the wayside and you are set free from anxiety.

Living life in the fast lane, or on auto-pilot, often prevents us spending time on something that is vital for human progression: solitude. Time given to thought does not separate us from the daily round, it plunges us more deeply into it. I remember a television interview with the poet Seamus Heaney in which he recalled a boyhood memory that inspired his poem 'Digging'. In his bedroom, he could hear his father digging potatoes outside. As he reflected on the effort involved, he felt that he wanted to spend his own life 'digging' with his pen. What emerged from that lifetime of reflective digging was a sublime collection of poetry and wisdom that garnered him a Nobel Prize – and a lasting legacy.

If Socrates's words inspire you and you want to 'know yourself' – dig more deeply – spend time with yourself. Learn to know and to believe not only in yourself, but in the meaning and purpose of humanity. The human adventure has yet to be played out. We are not yet done – there are always possibilities ahead of us.

What enabled those people who attempted to survive the horror of concentration camps during the Holocaust, and indeed what helps all of us in whatever we have to endure, is the thought that human life has meaning, however dim and distant it might seem, and our task is to search for it.

Viktor E. Frankl, a neuroscientist and psychologist, was imprisoned in Auschwitz, where his experiences of extreme human suffering enabled him to observe the crucial role of the mind – both in himself and other people. When everything else had been stripped away and the inmates had barely enough strength to stay alive, having been starved, mocked, beaten and deprived of every shred of human dignity, what often remained was their imagination – the ability to think beyond the suffering and to evoke memories of the world outside, of small everyday happenings and loved ones. The mind escaping into the past helped to maintain their hope of staying alive and someday reaching normality. Frankl describes all this, vividly and movingly, in his amazing book, *Man's Search For Meaning*:

> The intensification of inner life helped the prisoner find refuge from the emptiness, desolation and spiritual poverty of his existence, by letting him escape into the past … As the inner life of the prisoner became more intense he also experienced the beauty of art and nature as never before … How beautiful the world could be … The consciousness of one's inner value is anchored in higher, more spiritual things, and cannot be shaken by camp life.

13

Within You Without You

If I were asked to sum up this whole book in a few words, the lyrics from *Within You Without You* by the Beatles would be a strong contender, along with the quote from Dorothea Lynch right at the beginning. Both capture the essence of everything I am attempting to communicate here. So if you need a shortcut, it's on offer!

Some of the most profound and complex realities in human life are often summed up in the lyrics of popular songs. They are simple words that can communicate ideas more powerfully than complex analysis because, like poetry, they emanate from deep thought. The 1960s, when I was in my twenties, will always be a momentous time for me. In the midst of social upheaval and protest, there was a whole new atmosphere of hope and liberation: the colossus that was Martin Luther King Jr, who taught us that leadership and peaceful protest could change the world; the Nobel laureate Bob Dylan assuring us all that the times were indeed a-changin'. I think that same prize, the Nobel Prize for Literature, should be awarded to the Beatles, for their

outstanding contribution to music and art. The hallmark of
McCartney and Lennon's insightful lyrics was the inclusion
of profound and thoughtful perceptions of everyday life that,
enshrined in their music, reached millions all round the world.
A couple of years ago, I watched an amazing documentary in
which the musician and composer Howard Goodall analysed
the making of their ground-breaking album, *Sgt. Pepper's
Lonely Hearts Club Band*. He described it as not only 'a new
advance in sheer musical ambition and scope, but also the
most human of endeavours, firmly grounded in real life'.
More than that, he claimed the album was a game-changer
in the history of music. By using innovative techniques and
combining various musical influences from around the world
for the first time, the album set in motion what we would
now call 'world music'.

Along with *Sgt. Pepper*, the Beatles made another life-
changing contribution with their much-publicised trip to
India, which may have heralded a more reflective future
for the West. As the entire world tuned in to watch their
idols, they were, perhaps for the first time, en masse, exposed
to a culture of a spirituality that was natural in the Indian
continent. It would seem that from then on, the concept of
meditation began to gather momentum in the Western world.

George Harrison spent his entire life on a remarkable
spiritual journey. From early experiments with drugs and the
transcendental, his quest blossomed and became much more
grounded. In *Within You Without You*, his words are simple
and gentle, yet the way the great truths of life are expressed so
simply, all against a backdrop of expressive music that united
two continents, is genius. Goodall described it as: 'A heartfelt
reflection on the state of being in the modern world, and a
new kind of spirituality that many in the West were seeking'.

That's quite some statement, and a perceptive insight into what the modern world is seeking. What George Harrison in so few words managed to express was, if you like, a template not just for the spiritual life but for *all* of life.

I regularly listen to *Saturday Live* on Radio 4 while I'm getting ready to go to a football match. Each week, a guest chooses a piece of music they would like to pass on. The actor Stephen McGann chose *Within You Without You,* which he said made such an impression on him as a child that he bought his own son *Sgt. Pepper* and explained to him that the song contained life lessons. His favourite line 'when you've seen beyond yourself then you may find peace of mind is waiting there' – was, he said: 'Frankly, a good, simple, one-sentence message for life you could pass on to a young person or any person'.

Everything within this book is an attempt to expand on those gentle words. A deep spiritual life is not otherworldly or enigmatic. It is grounded in everyday life and happens on the inside as well as the outside.

At this point, I want to share my thoughts on the indelible words of the song, which I often go back to. However, copyright regulations prevent me from reproducing the lyrics, so I'm including my notes on them here. They powerfully express everything I believe:

In verse one: there is too much space between people – we're not close enough. If we try to hide or separate ourselves from others, it's just an illusion, an attempt to escape reality. We are all inextricably linked, but some people reach the end of their lives without knowing that.

The second verse refers to talking to friends about love and how we need to find it and share it – love shared between us all, he says, could save the world. He can see the truth and knows what life on Earth could be. For me, the evocative words 'if we only knew' sum up everything, as I share that deep conviction.

Verse three begins and ends within you: try to realise who you are and to discover your own depth and uniqueness – and that only you can bring about change in yourself. We are all small and humble, and this is the key to gaining understanding.

Verse four is a frustrated lament for the people who can't see further than personal gain. Love grows cold in them and their inner self somehow gets lost, without them ever seeing or knowing the beauty and truth of their existence.

Verse five talks about how finding your own centre sets you free to see the bigger picture beyond yourself, after which you will *know*. A time will come when we will all be united as one and peace of mind awaits us. I love the thought that when we realise that life goes on deep within us as well as without, we will discover peace of mind waiting right there.

14

Fortress Ego

I am a rock

Paul Simon

Ever since it was released in 1965, *The Paul Simon Songbook* has also been one of my favourite albums. I never tire of Paul Simon's voice, his insightful lyrics and the single guitar accompaniment. He is a massively talented poet, songwriter and musician, and one of my favourite songs from that album is *I Am a Rock*. This plaintive song must have been about lost love, friendship or betrayal. Simon's remedy was emphatic: enforced isolation was the only thing that could help with heartache. But while this experience of pain, which all of us undergo at some time or other, may need a cocoon of self-protection, it can only ever be temporary. As a poet, I think he was defiantly disclaiming another great poet, John Donne, who wrote: 'No man is an island, entire of itself.' A kind of rhetorical 'yes he is!'

At that moment, Paul Simon is determined to map out his future, which would not include other people who may inflict pain – he would be enclosed and protected in his fortress. We know absolutely how he feels because, again, we've all been there, and we therefore know that it can only ever be a temporary escape while we recover.

I Am a Rock might be very meaningful to someone going through trauma, but it also has wider implications: it is highlighting what is an impossible way to live and, while it exaggerates, it also skilfully exposes what's wrong in the world. People need people – pain can only ever be healed by others. Being so isolated and autonomous leads to separateness and egoism, which is what hides behind all discord, factions, wars and destructive forces: the desire to be isolated, to go it alone and seek fulfilment by solitary effort and adopt the mantra 'everyone for themselves'.

This sad, sombre spectacle is not confined to individuals. At its most dangerous, it has various groups, societies and nations under its spell, all of whom are under the illusion of being singled out and set apart from the rest – hence the insidious scourge of racism.

In order to focus on the implications of egoism, we must make a distinction, because the word 'ego' is sometimes misinterpreted. Ego means 'self', something pure and good; each of us has a natural, very sound instinct that compels us to embrace life and be fulfilled. What gets in the way and distorts it is egocentrism and self-centredness. The egoist has no conception of team. Attempting to go it alone and cutting ourselves off from others is against nature, and often sadly a result of insecurity.

If we look back to pre-human life, we could say that egoism is a sort of hangover from the brutal forces of positive selection, when all elements were vying in the struggle for existence. Yet when animal life became human, we were gifted a conscious mind, after which we figure out that humans turning towards each other and joining forces was always going to be a better bet for survival. But, mindful of our history – and the state of our world – we are still far from having worked that one out. We see egoism is rife, and there are many shades of it every day: how many times have we heard the expression 'it's all about him or her'? If that person happens to be a world leader, it becomes the most dangerous form of egoism, fanned by what Nietzsche called 'the will to power', which is power over others. All over the world, right at this moment, the most powerful egoists are giving orders to torture, deprive or kill other humans. Gun crime, knife crime, countries being obliterated and millions of families with small children left homeless... Future generations, having hopefully matured, will surely view us as barbarians.

The challenge for the future wellbeing of the world is to work out the root cause of egoism, learn how to deal with it and integrate it into our education systems. One plausible theory involves a tiny four-letter word: *fear.* Paul Simon's remedy for heartache is rooted in fear. Inside our own fortress, behind all the bravado, there's a massive cover-up going on – we are hiding out of fear. Fear of being rejected, of not achieving, not being important or powerful, a fear of pain and fear of love, of friendship or of not being liked, a multitude of varying levels of fear all hidden away inside our fortress.

Franklin D. Roosevelt, in his inaugural address to the American people in 1933, really hit the spot with his much-quoted line: 'Let me assert my firm belief that the only thing we have to fear is fear itself.' The implications of those insightful words, spoken by the world's most powerful leader, had a lasting legacy. But there's more: addressing Congress in 1941, he spoke of a future world founded on freedom; freedom of speech and belief, freedom from want and freedom from fear. If we think of what freedom feels like, living without fear must surely be top of the list. Roosevelt's vision of the things that matter in life included the wellbeing of the whole world – nothing isolationist or egotistical about 'making America great'. His intelligent, clear perception was that America being great would depend on how the future of the whole world unfolded.

There can't be many of us who haven't had to do battle with fear and anxiety, and it's not of our making. We are all victims of circumstances, outside pressures and expectations that can give a crushing sense of inadequacy. For me, failing my eleven-plus, enduring the taunts from my peers on their way to the much-coveted grammar school and facing my family's disappointment was hard going. I was just eleven, but I already felt like one of life's failures. The fear of failure and external influences that put pressure on us, making demands we cannot fulfil, can trigger a life of perpetual anxiety.

If we go deeper, we discover that the root of fear is an inner fragility. Human beings are fragile, sensitive and sometimes afraid. Wanting to overcome that and be fulfilled as a person is a sound instinct, and there are some astonishingly effective ways of learning how to deal with fear. The prime one is knowing and valuing yourself as a person. Accept that being sensitive and fragile is part of being human and that covering it up with egoism never works in the end. Logically, the way to overcome fear is to become inwardly strong. How to achieve this is the remedy that runs through this book: knowing and understanding ourselves, our own desires, our possibilities and potential, free from outside influences and pressures. Everyone is unique and has something to offer the rest.

On this particular point, two people are lodged in my memory. The late Sir David Frost, who spent his life interviewing celebrities, said that, without exception, every person he met was special and had something others didn't. Norman Parkinson, a famous photographer in the 1950s and 1960s, was once asked in an interview: 'What happens when you have to photograph someone who isn't beautiful? How do you tackle that?' His reply? 'It's never happened – when I look at someone through a lens, I always see something of beauty in every person.'

The old adage 'fortune favours the brave' always holds good. One way to combat fear is not to run for cover but to run in the opposite direction, into the light; instead of fearing 'fear itself', we should be brave and face it. Hiding from fear means pretending to be big, so the opposite is not minding being small. Be happy to be wrong. People who think they are never wrong are walking adverts for egoism. Rejecting egoism means acknowledging that it's perfectly okay to be wrong and make mistakes. And the key thing – and I think this is where the bravery really kicks in – is in not being *afraid to fail.* Why are we pressured into thinking we must not fail?

Fear can have no truck with someone who is happy to fail. Being willing to fail releases us from many expectations and anxieties. A wonderful thing then happens: there's no pressure – sometimes you succeed and sometimes you don't, and a new freedom comes into play. I may well, in spite of every effort, do or say the wrong thing, forget such and such and, just like the rest of the human race, *make mistakes,* but if I'm willing to fail, fear is utterly defeated and leaves me at peace.

I can give you a personal example of that. Publishers often ask their authors to do book signings, and so I found myself, one grey, damp morning in Leeds, positioned on the ground floor of a very large branch of Boots. Absolutely no one was buying cookery books that day. So I sat for one hour, listening to intermittent announcements: 'Today we have Delia Smith signing copies of her book' … 'Don't forget Delia Smith is signing her book on our ground floor today!' All the time, I was just wishing I was! Every now and then, someone would ask me if I knew where the corn plasters or some other item was, and afterwards, the book buyer was at great pains to assure me that the weather or the time of day had been the problem, not realising that it just didn't matter to me. I had learned from many other failed book signings that, in truth, it wasn't a problem – I still giggle when I remember the time a bookshop hired the same bodyguard for me that they had used to protect Gordon Ramsay, only for the poor man to watch me sign copies for six people and a dog! There will always be shades of egoism in all of us, but being as free of it as possible and able to have a laugh is much less draining.

Abraham H. Maslow, the famous American psychologist, said we have much to learn from small children because they are free from being influenced. Recently, I watched a twelve-month-old baby taking his first steps, while the grown-ups around him were all chatting. The polished wooden floor was quite slippery and his feet were bare, but no matter; one, two or three wobbly steps, then down. Unaware he was being watched and using his hands to ease himself back up onto his feet, he just carried on, repeating the process and ignoring what must have been quite hard bumps as he went down, quite unconscious of each *failed* attempt. Undeterred, he continued without fear, determined that nothing was going to stop him taking more and more steps and learning how to walk. It was the perfect cameo of human life. There are always bumpy or slippery roads, but the possibility of being able to walk freely without fear, and to walk tall by being inwardly strong, is a whole lot better than living in a lonely fortress.

15

As Yet Unresolved

From a purely positivistic point of view, the human being is the most mysterious and disconcerting of subjects science has encountered. In fact, we must admit that science has not yet found a place for the human in its descriptions of the universe ... Science, in its present reconstructions of the world, fails to grasp an essential factor or, to be more exact – an entire dimension – of the universe.

Teilhard de Chardin

It would seem that the answer to our original question, 'What is human life?', has not as yet been fully resolved by science. How did life come about? Not yet known. Do humans have universal significance? So far, none. Does our species have a future? Sadly not, because all things come to an end.

Even if it is true that in knowing the human we might find the solution to all that we *can* know, we will only ever arrive at that point if we persist in finding out. Everyone has a role to play in this. The fact that we are still so mysterious means that anything is possible. This is both challenging and intriguing, since we all already have a great deal of lived expertise. None of us asked to be born into this world, but we were, and we all share the day-to-day experience. And it's only through this that we can understand our presence within the world and *collectively* find the answers.

For me, Teilhard's words bear this out: 'To understand the world knowledge is not enough; you must see it, touch it, live in its presence.' And because that applies to all of us and not just the experts, everyone's experience counts and every one of us has our own take on it – and it's in that everyday encountering that the sheer wonder of it all emerges. From the traveller, the gardener and the winemaker, to the farmer, the engineer and the astronaut gazing in awe at the Earth from space. That housekeeper I met in intensive care, who said, while mopping the floor: 'I so love my work because I feel I'm making a contribution to the amazing work that goes on here.' And so she was.

There are an incalculable number of daily occupations that put us in touch with what surrounds us, end to end, top to bottom, which is the ever-varying aspects of the beauty and wonder of our world and our place in it. Human beings are not just in the world, but *of* the world and are the key players in its preservation and progress. So many millions of people have lived and struggled to interpret the world, and all have played a part in its development.

Anyone who has been fortunate enough to see the BBC documentary series *Civilisations* – either the original or the 2018 version – could not fail to be in awe at how human life on Earth has unfolded – the drama, the colour, the ongoing progress of civilisation after civilisation. Great works of art depict people, landscapes and architecture, reflecting how they have lived, worked and left their mark on the centuries. At every point there has been a sense of quest and of movement, as art and culture cross continents, unbound by the constrictions of nation and race. And all through this we sense that beyond the terrifying and cruel aspects of our history, at base there is still a human dignity and a cohesion in our collective strivings and aspirations.

Yet still the question: what is human life? A species unlike any other, existing on a planet unlike any other, courtesy of an immense and mysterious matrix. The human is unique, distinguished from all other forms of life by its large brain and fully conscious reflective mind. Every person is playing their own part in this amazing adventure we call human life.

The passage below, from *The Human Phenomenon* by Teilhard de Chardin, takes us back to our origins, when evolution reached the crucial step of giving birth to humanity. What makes it momentous and emotive is when we compare it with what had gone before. Billions and billions of years of slowly evolving forms of life, and then that hallowed moment and the *culmination* of all that had gone before:

From the organic point of view, it comes down to the question of a better brain. But how did this cerebral perfecting take place – how could it have functioned – unless a whole series of other conditions had been realised together at precisely the same time? If the living being the human was born of had not been a biped, its hands would not have been free in time enough to relieve the jaws of their prehensile function, and as a result the thick band of maxillary muscles that imprisoned the skull would not have been relaxed. Thanks to bipedalism freeing the hands the brain could enlarge; and thanks to that at the same time the eyes,

drawing near to each other on the diminished face, could
begin to converge and fix their gaze on what the hands
took hold of, brought near, and, in every sense of the
word, presented: The very act of reflection, exteriorised!
In itself there is nothing surprising in this marvellous
conjunction. Is not the smallest thing formed in the
world in this way always the fruit of an incredible
coincidence – a knot of fibres running together forever
from the four corners of space? Life works not by
following an isolated thread or by starting over again.
It pushes its whole net ahead at the same time. This is
how the embryo is formed in the womb that bears it. We
should have known. And this is precisely why we should
feel some satisfaction in recognising that the human
being was born under the same maternal law.

16

Why Evolution?

True physics is that which will someday succeed in integrating the totality of the human being into a coherent representation of the world … The human is not the static centre of the world we once thought for so long but the axis and arrow of evolution, which is much more beautiful.

Teilhard de Chardin

Once you pose the question: 'Why is human life?' as we did in Chapter 5, along come other innumerable 'whys'; not least the emotive question of evolution. If humanity is to offer a 'coherent representation of the world', evolution is going to be pivotal in reaching any kind of understanding. Darwin's seminal work, *On the Origin of Species*, dramatically reshaped our thinking, but it also brought shock waves, fierce debate and, in some quarters, emphatic denial; even now, there's massive disagreement on issues concerning evolution.

On a personal level, while I am quite certain that evolution is central to understanding life, I can also get quite emotional reading the intensely moving first chapter of the

Book of Genesis, which, although allegorical, is a literary masterpiece. Somehow it manages to vividly capture the drama and the beauty of the whole phenomenon of life on Earth. And, together with the painting depicting these words on the ceiling of the Sistine Chapel, both writer and artist were simply human beings, attempting to express their awe and wonder at how life came to be.

I want to return to the bigger question here: not *what* evolution is, but *why* is it? On a cosmic scale, this is a hugely significant question since, as we've said, so far the Earth is the only planet we know of with precisely the right conditions for any kind of life to exist. Without specific facts, perhaps one approach in attempting to figure it out is to use the imagination.

Imagine that we were somewhere outside the cosmos, on some outpost where futuristic technology is able to offer an overview of all that exists. Everything. First, we would be utterly overwhelmed at such an awesome spectacle. Space, and the sheer immensity of the universe, now not imagined but an undisputed reality. Packed with stars and planets, including some giants 150 times the size of our sun and others that are tiny by comparison, some existing four billion light years away. Yet seen from the Earth with the naked eye, the twinkling lights of the stars communicate a kind of reassuring friendliness. From pre-history to modern day, the stars in the night sky have provided humans, animals, even some migratory birds and spawning fish with an infallible means of navigation, which suggests a natural cohesion between life on Earth and the universe.

Next on our imaginary outpost, try to visualise zooming in on our own galaxy and solar system. While the Sun and the Moon are obviously the key players, 100 billion stars silently encircle the tiny Earth like a celestial comfort zone. Zoom in again to the Earth's surface – it's right here that 3 to 4 million years ago, the first stirrings of the biological evolution of every form of living, breathing life was set in motion. There may be dissent about the detail, but looking from the outside, could there be any reaction other than emotion and awe?

How did it happen? What was it that prompted those first primordial stirrings and initiated the genesis of life on Earth? And even more significantly, why was it that at a certain point, after a long gestation, the mechanics of evolution radically changed? Over thousands of centuries, varying species developed – or became extinct. Then, all of a sudden, evolution changed course and made an unprecedented leap, as something totally unique and exceptional emerged: the human phenomenon. The ultimate species. A summary from then might start with the discovery of fire and the invention of the wheel, then fast forward and here we are, walking on the Moon and launching powerful telescopes to explore space – next stop, Mars. Humans not only have the world at their feet but the surrounding cosmos, just waiting to be penetrated. We're still evolving after all those years, except that now, it's our collective consciousness and powers of reasoning that are charting our progress.

Again on the imaginary outpost, does it not seem likely that some kind of meaningful universal quest is unfolding here on Earth, and might it provide an explanation for the question: *why* is evolution? Is the phenomenon we call human life about something, or is it just a cosmic accident, a chance happening, with confused humanity progressing yet, at the same time, drifting towards a meaningless and uncertain future – or, at worst, oblivion?

This, of course, is *the* fundamental question, and so far, no scientific explanation of life on Earth has been given. It's also the one big question that sharply divides us, from those who emphatically insist we are utterly insignificant, to those who are merely indifferent, while on the other side of the divide there are those who, through their own reflective experiences of life and thought, are quite certain – or at least open to the idea – that the presence of human life *does* have meaning and purpose.

Teilhard de Chardin passionately believed that humanity *is* evolution, its axis and its arrow, and that it is *we ourselves* who are responsible for how life on Earth – however slowly and imperceptibly – continues to evolve. In spite of chaos and unresolved conflict, he believed that humanity is undergoing what he wonderfully described as 'a process of becoming'. It's not there yet, but it's moving towards something better.

Evolution is an emotive subject and there is much more to say, but for now I want to share a beautiful and poetic allegory of evolution which, from the outside looking in, sums it up perfectly. It's taken from one of Teilhard's essays, 'Notes on Progress;.

> The day on which the first voice rang out, crying
> to humanity peacefully slumbering on the raft of
> the Earth, 'We are moving! We are going forward!'
> Humanity divided to its very depths into two irrevocably
> opposed camps – one looking towards the horizon and
> proclaiming … 'We are moving' and the other, without
> shifting its position, obstinately maintaining 'Nothing
> changes. We are not moving at all.'
>   These latter 'immobilists', though they lack passion,
> have common sense on their side, habit of thought,

inertia, pessimism and also to some extent, mortality and religion. Nothing, they argue, has changed since humanity began to hand down the memory of the past; not the undulations of the Earth, or the forms of life, or the genius of humanity or even its goodness ... For the sake of human tranquillity, in the name of fact, and in defence of the sacred established order, the immobilists forbid the Earth to move. Nothing changes, they say, or can change. The raft must drift purposelessly on a shoreless sea.

But the other half of humanity, startled by the lookout's cry, has left the huddle where the rest of the crew sit with their heads together, telling time-honoured tales. Gazing out over the dark sea, they study the lapping water along the hull of the craft that bears them, breathe the scents borne on the breeze and gaze at the shadows cast from pole to pole by a changeless eternity. And all these things, while remaining separate – the ripple of the water, the scent of the air, the lights in the sky – become linked together and acquire a new sense: the fixed, random universe is seen to move.

17

Convergence: Evolution's U-Turn

The direction of travel, however gropingly, of human evolution's leading edge is towards convergence ... Reflective consciousness has been evolving at an ever-increasing rate from its emergence and is changing the balance ... While the aggressive competitive instinct remains a powerful but gradually decreasing force shaping human evolution, it has been countered by an increasing comprehension that peaceful cooperation is the only way for the human species to evolve.

John Hands, *Cosmosapiens*

What an amazing piece of writing! I still want to cheer out loud when someone wiser or more qualified than me affirms everything I believe.

John Hands has been described as an 'astute observer of recent trends in scientific ideas, bold enough to point out what he sees as sense and nonsense and intelligently explain why', and this is a fitting description of his remarkable book, which took ten years of research. In it, he evaluates

scientific theories on human evolution, from the origin of
the universe to the present day, exploring the same questions
about human existence. Who are we? Why are we? Why are
we here? In the above quote, he has managed to capture not
just the essence of human evolution, but its pivotal role in
helping to find the answers.

The Darwinian revolution – or should we say 'revelation'? –
left in its wake a string of diverse theories and strongly held
opinions. He has a devoted following of neo-Darwinists
and ultra-Darwinists and he's even sometimes crowned
the patron saint of secularism, but not everyone worships
at his imaginary shrine. One scientist, Michael Polanyi,
believed that, for almost two centuries, Darwinism, while
investigating the conditions of evolution, has completely
overlooked its action: diverting attention from – and offering
no explanation for – how a material system can become a
conscious responsible person. Or, indeed, how it explained
the arrival of humanity and its continued development over
thousands of years. Put simply, it is that movement that
underlines the true reality of evolution.

Leaving aside those who can't accept that evolution
actually happens, the Darwinian interpretation is something
called 'natural selection'. During the 4 billion years that pre-
human life evolved, it appeared that everything happened
by way of blind random chance, and that the emergence
of life involved the activity of primordial genes vying with
one another for existence. This all turned out to be rather
brutal. The strongest and fittest survived, while the rest went
to the wall. So we see the emergence of life as evolving by
way of competitive combat and everything ends up being
innately selfish – a pretty bleak picture. But evolution is, first
and foremost, about movement and progress, and what also

emerges is, thankfully, evidence of an equally natural instinct for cooperation.

As the evolutionary epic unfolds, a unique species bursts on to the scene: homo sapiens – 'wise people' – and with their appearance on Earth, life undergoes a momentous change. Instinct blossoms into an intelligent, reflective consciousness that will generate the continuing movement of life. Thinking minds become capable of reasoning how to not just survive, but to progress and acquire *knowledge*. In gaining knowledge (which includes self-knowledge) instinctive, intuitive humans become able to think things through and become sensitised to extra dimensions of their existence – if they choose to. We all have the choice between sticking with the selfish genes ('every one for themselves') and being attentive to an emerging inner spirit of goodness and ingenuity, which then begins to drive the inner forces of evolving life and orchestrate the human future. Not accidental and random but reasoned and purposeful – given, of course, that evolution, like all good things, takes time.

We can imagine how the first thinking humans began to realise that self-serving, competitive instincts were not going be the best bet for survival. Perhaps a group of cave dwellers shared a campfire and began to understand the logic of progression would involve joining forces – after all, other species had begun to work that out. Flocks of birds, shoals of fish and even insects understand collaboration. Think of a pride of lions on a hunt: as soon as supper has been sighted, the attack involves a group working together; one very obvious life lesson for lions, and for humans, is that the only way you get to eat is by working as a *team*.

So the story unfolds. Humans band together into groups – some of them itinerant – gradually expanding, multiplying and migrating across the Earth's surface. Nations, continents and empires emerge, followed by much brutal combat and endless territorial conflicts. Yet perhaps the grip of isolationist egoism on the world is showing signs of moving towards its peak. The Black Lives Matter movement and the protests in Hong Kong, Thailand, Belarus and Myanmar are all signs of the times. Could it be that the last century, which endured two devastating world wars and the atomic bomb, has left its mark on humankind and, at some level, all this marks the beginning of a turning point? Is it not now obvious that egoism is at the root of all dissension and what leads to wars?

In the end, egoism will be no match for the ever-emerging movement of the cooperating human spirit because this, just as in those two wars, is what turned out to be the stronger element. And this is what, in those perilous moments, inspired the whole world to *join forces* and, however narrowly, finally triumph. People of all nationalities collaborated in a common cause, sacrificing their lives and sharing the burdens. Everywhere there was selflessness, risk, bravery and determination, which surely shows something of the innermost truth of our existence. Those who experienced it may feel a certain nostalgia for how it touched them, but what those who sacrificed their lives could not have known is that they not only won our freedom but may have helped to change the direction of the world.

Witness the formation of the United Nations by fifty-one countries in 1945, in order to maintain peace and promote international cooperation. And in 1951, the battered countries of post-war Europe had the idea that if they could work together, they might avoid such devastating atrocities occurring again. Sixty years later, in 2012, the European Union was awarded the Nobel Peace Prize for contributing to the advancement of 'peace, reconciliation, democracy and human rights in Europe'.

The EU continues to be a great success, and I was devastated when my own country narrowly voted to leave the EU and go in the opposite direction. I still feel a personal sense of loss that we are not part of that vision of the future and I applaud the EU's spirit of cooperation. Isolationist nationalism is never going to work since it's against evolution. And unless we stop the increasing threat of climate change, nations will eventually be forced to unite when the whole world may be facing a shortage of water!

Faltering first steps, perhaps, but the post-war formation of the UN and the EU was the beginning of a significant movement towards cooperation in the human future. There's still the turmoil of tyrannical regimes and egoist isolationists, but all that will eventually be no match for a cooperating world. The evolution of human life on Earth may take eons, but it will always have the last word. Nothing can prevent humans from eventually knowing and believing in themselves and discovering that the greatest energy emanates from unity, with, as John Hands says, 'an increasing comprehension that peaceful cooperation is the only way for the human species to evolve'.

PART TWO

None of us is as Smart as all of Us

18

The Evolution of a Person

One could say that we seem to have lost the sense of the true nature of person along with our respect for it...

Teilhard de Chardin, *The Human Phenomenon*

Because you are doing the best you can (though you may sometimes fail), you are forming your own self within the world, and you are helping the world to form itself around you.

Teilhard de Chardin, *Letters From a Traveller*

Teilhard called his most famous book *The Human Phenomenon* and, for me, this book comes closer to conveying what that means than anything written before or since. As the cultural historian Thomas Berry concluded, 'there is no substitute for a close reading of this work'. And in the foreword to the most recent translation of the book, the evolutionary cosmologist Brian Swimme wrote: 'The book you now hold is because the universe has laboured for billions of years to reach a point in its complexification where it can now bring forth something new through you. It comes to you with its own ideas for your future, for what is needed now for the universe's unfolding story is not a new galaxy or a new star. What is needed is a new form of human being.' Could anything be more exhilarating, thought-provoking or challenging?

Teilhard ends his own preface to the book with these words: 'I do not see how it is possible for anyone to give a full and coherent representation of the human phenomenon' – the reality of human life was so overwhelming that he had to admit that certain aspects were incommunicable. Yet his life's mission was to try to share his deep insights into what it means to be a human and to guide us through fears and false perspectives in order to form new eyes.

Once the immensity of time and space and the conditions of the universe were comprehended, planet Earth, with its cargo of life, came to be regarded by some scientists as a freak manifestation. I recall Stephen Hawking saying that he was 'extremely grateful' for life. How could he write off his own great mind and his contribution to science as being part of some irrelevant cosmic accident?

Teilhard took the opposite view: it was precisely *because* of its unlikely presence within the universe that life on Earth had to be of vital and momentous significance. The tiny planet, positioned within such a specific planetary arrangement and mysteriously fit for purpose, led him to conclude that life on Earth was not only extremely significant but central to all that exists. 'The truth of the human being *is* the truth of the universe,' he said. 'We humans cannot see ourselves completely except as part of humanity, humanity as part of life, and life as part of the universe.' Throughout his writings, he is at great pains to emphasise that last sentence. He also believed passionately that every individual is 'a child of the Earth and a citizen of the universe'.

It is strange that what is not yet known is not much spoken about, particularly as, so far, science does not yet have an adequate explanation for the appearance of life. For me, the scientist Francis Crick had the best explanation: 'An honest man, armed with all the knowledge available to us now, could only state that, in some sense, the origin of life appears at the moment to be almost a miracle, so many are the conditions which would have had to be satisfied to get it going.'

Nor, indeed, can it be explained why it is that, within all life, only the human species is gifted the mysterious presence of thought, intelligence and an evolving consciousness. The progress of the past bears witness to this phenomenon. Humanity's continued existence has meant continued learning, and only knowledge can answer the most challenging questions of existence: humans figuring out what we are and why we are present in the universe.

What is absolutely central to everything is the fact that each one of us is utterly unique, both physically and consciously. This, whichever way you look at it, is phenomenal. Each of us has inherited the natural potential to become *someone*, and every *one* of us has the freedom – and the responsibility – to develop our own unique personality, starting as an individual and ending as a fully evolved person – and each one important to the whole! Yet from the word go, unlike some other species, it's impossible for a human to be self-sufficient – a newborn baby left to itself can't survive. It needs nurturing, feeding, parental guidance, family and friendship. But more important than that, it will spend its whole life engaging with others. This is vital because we now know that humans are social beings that can *only* develop in association with one another. We all have multiple instances in our lives when other people enable us to discover something in ourselves that we didn't know was there. And we all know that humans tend to be at their best when they are involved in and part of a team or a community.

The real challenge for humans is self-belief, both at a personal level and as a species. We must become alert to the network of information that helps each of us uncover our own personality, not just as part of a uniform mass but each of us, in association with others, being enabled by those associations to rise to our full potential.

Human life is such an overwhelmingly awesome reality that we can be afraid to contemplate its amazing implications. Yet life is all about ceaseless discovery and movement. The whole world is in the process of being born, and each of us has a unique part to play. The moment we can even vaguely accept this, there will be an added passion and a new sense of purpose in our lives. We can't possibly know all the answers yet – we're still evolving. But as Teilhard says: 'The immediate question is not one of knowing precisely where the current is taking us and how shall we shoot the rapids, but simply of deciding to jump in, follow the main course of the stream and discover the current.' It's hard to believe that anyone would want to turn that down.

In 2017, I attended a course in Cambridge organised by the Faraday Institute for Science and Religion. I had read a brilliant book by one of the lecturers – Simon Conway Morris, a professor of evolutionary paleobiology. *Life's Solution: Inevitable Humans In a Lonely Universe* is written for scientists, but I found it accessible, humorous and deeply profound. The following is taken from the book:

The heart of the problem, I believe, is to explain how
it might be that we, a product of evolution, possess an
overwhelming sense of purpose and moral identity, yet
arose by processes that were seemingly without meaning.
If, however, we can begin to demonstrate that organic
evolution contains deeper structures and potentialities,
if not inevitabilities, then perhaps we can begin to move
away from the dreary materialism of much current
thinking … In my opinion, the sure sign of the right
road is a limitless prospect of deeper knowledge: what
was once baffling is now clear, what seemed absurdly
important is now simply childish, yet still the journey is
unfinished.

19

A Sense of Species

Nothing ... can weed out the feeling of human solidarity, deeply lodged in man's understanding and heart ... A person is appealed to be guided in his acts ... by the perception of his oneness with each human being. In the practice of human mutual aid, which we can trace to the earliest beginnings of evolution, we thus find the positive and undoubted origins of our ethical conceptions; and we can affirm that the ethical progress of humanity, mutual support not mutual struggle, has had the leading part. In its wide extension, even in the present time, we also see the best guarantee of a still loftier evolution of our race.

Peter Kropotkin, *Mutual Aid: A Factor of Evolution*

How strange it is that concepts that are deeply lodged in our understanding are so hidden that when they do surface, it's as if they were staring us in the face all the time. Or, as we used to say, 'the penny drops'. What we are attempting to uncover is a profound instinct, common to all and rooted in our deepest being, that is often hidden. When fully apprehended, it has implications that are not only life-changing, but world-changing.

Peter Kropotkin was a Russian scientist who was born in 1822. Having been inspired by Darwin's *On the Origin of Species*, he set out, aged twenty, to study both human and animal life, beginning in eastern Siberia and northern Manchuria. He began to uncover evidence that Darwin's original evolutionary hypothesis, which he so much admired, had been distorted by his followers. *Mutual Aid* is an enchanting book if you are a lover of nature; he observes 'animal life in abundance which passed before my very eyes … mutual aid and mutual support … which was important to the maintenance of life, the preservation of each species, and its further evolution'. A far cry from the 'combat and survival of the fittest' interpretation of ultra-Darwinists, he could not see that 'to admit a pitiless inner war for life in each species, and to see in that war a condition of progress, was to admit something which not only had not yet been proved, but also lacked confirmation from direct observation'.

From then on, Kropotkin engaged in a lifelong investigation that led him to conclude that, while life is certainly a struggle that only the toughest survive, this does not always happen through selfish combat and competition. Instead, he closely observed that cooperation played a significantly greater part in the survival of species. His book has become a fitting testament to this research and was described as 'one of the world's greatest books'.

Early on in the book, Kropotkin recalls a conversation that had inspired him between Johann Peter Eckermann, a zoologist, and the literary giant Johann Wolfgang von Goethe. Two fledgling wrens had escaped Eckermann and he recalled finding them in a robin's nest the next day, being fed by the parents. Goethe reacted excitedly, 'If it be true that this feeding of a stranger goes through all of nature, as something having the character of a general law – then many an enigma would be solved.' Quite a statement. The idea of a natural support system running through all of life has huge implications: hidden behind the chaos that works against nature, he had discovered a hidden natural mutual affinity. Kropotkin took up the challenge, spending the rest of his life attempting to solve the mysteries of mutual support.

Kropotkin could not have foreseen that, almost two centuries later, there would be a consensus – and indeed, a general law – that mutual support does go 'through all of nature'. The word used by evolutionary scientists is 'convergence'. There is now evidence among all living creatures – birds, animals, insects and marine life, as well as humans – that in the struggle for survival, mutual aid and cooperation plays a part. Scientists have even discovered underground mutual networks that enable trees to distribute support to one another. And this newly acquired knowledge is revealing how nature's support systems are actually being destroyed by deforestation, intensive farming and the destruction of ecosystems. Plants, animals and other organisms naturally *work together* to support what can only be called 'the miracle of life', and humans who are *not working together* are now actually tearing it apart. To echo Greta Thunberg's comment at the 2019 Climate Action Summit: 'How dare you.'

We are now able to witness the quest for the survival of life on our planet in our own homes, through television. In Britain, the best-known programmes are those of the BBC Bristol film crews who work alongside Sir David Attenborough. We can observe at close quarters the amazing struggle for existence and marvel at the selfless parenting and mutual cooperation between creatures, even in the depths of the ocean. For me, the emperor penguins will always stand out as the most dramatic and moving example. In an attempt to keep warm in a hostile Antarctic storm, with icy winds, driving snow and life-threatening conditions, the penguins formed concentric circles, tightly packed together. This meant the backs of those on the outside of the circle took the brunt of it, while protecting those on the inside. Every so often, the inside ones would change places with the outer circle, in an attempt to ensure an equal chance of survival for all. Sir David Attenborough was astonished, saying: 'I have never seen a finer example of cooperation.'

This is a far cry from the pessimistic and downbeat theories of selfish genes and fierce competition. It's also a reality that we live with on a daily basis: people help one another. It may not be in our genes, but it continues to evolve in our deepest consciousness, and it is quite true that nothing can 'weed out human solidarity, deeply lodged in our understanding and heart'.

Everything always leads back to the inside of things. What is lodged deep in our understanding, a natural part of what we are, should give us cause for hope. We may live in a superficial fog of turmoil and fear, yet what we have within us is an established reality. Kropotkin's research, so clearly demonstrated by the penguins, is being affirmed by evolutionary science.

The implications of this are momentous. We humans, the culmination of four billion years of evolving life, have to conclude that our future survival, and the way to tackle climate change and build a better world, will have to involve greater global cooperation. Not as a uniform mass but with each person, group or nation retaining their own identity, while at the same time recognising a sense of belonging to and having allegiance with the whole. It's very simple and obvious. The idea of any one nation being greater than the rest or of retaining national sovereignty is simply outdated, and neither can nations falsely insulate themselves from what continually threatens our existence: nuclear weapons, climate change and the scourge of inequality. There is only one possible solution: human beings have to join forces. This is not a utopian pipedream or some contemporary whim – it's as plain as day. If we can believe in the bigger picture and get a sense of ourselves as a species, we will then achieve in union with one another 'the best guarantee of a still loftier evolution of our race'.

20

Solidarity: The Hidden Adhesive

My acceptance is not indifference or helplessness. I feel deep moral indignation at a regime that treats human beings in such a way … When I say it doesn't really matter if I go or someone else does, the main thing is that so many thousands have to go. It is not as if I want to fall into the arms of destruction with a resigned smile – far from it … But I don't think I would feel happy if I were exempted from what so many others have to suffer … I know whatever I may have to give to others, I can give no matter where I am – here in the circle of my friends or over there in a concentration camp. And it is sheer ignorance to think oneself too good to share the fate of the masses.

Etty Hillesum

Etty Hillesum, a young Jewish woman who died at Auschwitz in 1943, wrote those words after refusing to go into hiding in Amsterdam, during the Nazi occupation of the Netherlands. It is remarkable that in the midst of the most terrifying circumstances, she was able to stand shoulder to shoulder with others and share in their suffering. How it is that this human solidarity surfaces even in grave circumstances is a mystery, but it is by no means unusual.

Another example, this time from someone on the receiving end, was that of Ant Middleton, a member of the elite Special Boat Service and a much-lauded member of the military. He was out, as he had been many times before, on a highly dangerous mission tracking a Taliban leader, Ant was point man, which means 'first man in' (later the title of his bestselling autobiography). As he was poised, ready to kick down the door and enter, his team behind him, bullets flying through the door, he found that, for the first time ever, he couldn't move or overcome the acute fear that had suddenly gripped him. Waiting until the next pause in the machine gun fire, he tried again but still froze.

Then something happened that he would never forget. It was a moment so intense he would be unable to recall it 'without getting goosebumps'. All that happened was that the man behind him squeezed his shoulder. No words, but what he was saying was, 'I know what you're feeling – I'm here with you to either take the bullet or finish the job.' Like a flash, the fear left and he felt invincible: 'I can remember thinking, when the chips are down, when you're at the lowest ever, when you're staring death in the eyes; that's when teamwork counts – you know you have people alongside you who are *naturally* committed to you.'

It's the word *naturally* that is so significant. We all know it's there: it pops up all the time in our daily lives, rarely making headlines, but there's a gentle, if often hidden, undercurrent of caring inherent in human nature. Cooperation and a respect for life is not something we learn from the outside – it's intrinsic to our DNA. The learning comes in *recognising* that it's there.

All the wars, factions and turmoil in the world come from us failing to sense this fundamental reality. Having enemies and destroying one another is, in terms of evolution, juvenile. Now that we are maturing, more connected through technology and engaging in more grown-up, joined-up thinking, a natural cohesion is beginning to surface. Perhaps we are starting to realise that a unified effort to change things is more powerful than what divides us. We can see this in the young people who are, perhaps more acutely than some, sensing the signs of the times and agitating for change. Greta Thunberg rightly grabbed the headlines, but there are millions like her who understand the gravity of climate change and feel compelled to do something.

Ultimately, there is no such thing as 'blood relatives'; we all have the same blood coursing through our veins. We are part of the same species connected by a solidarity that is becoming more and more visible. Every now and then, we are reminded of this when millions of people around the world engage in something that unites them at a deep level, even if only briefly: the Thai cave rescue that hit the headlines in 2018 was a perfect example. Twelve young footballers and their coach were trapped in caves by fast-rising waters for three weeks. At home we, along with the rest of the world, were testing our optimism to the limit, daring to hope in what seemed like an impossible situation. A *Guardian* editorial captured what was so incredible about the rescue:

> What made this story so powerful and absorbing was seeing humanity at its best: this is a tale of innocence protected; of perseverance against the odds and heroism in the face of danger; above all, of triumph over despair. It speaks to us unusually strongly now, as the antithesis

of all we see around us. The boys themselves, with their coach's encouragement, have shown extraordinary fortitude. At a moment of rising division, the rescue has been a model of international collaboration. US military personnel, British rescue experts and specialists from China, Australia and Japan have worked alongside the Thai authorities and people. In an era of greed, many involved are unpaid volunteers … The rescue is a true inspiration: a powerful reminder of what can be done when humans overcome their fears, pull together and put others first. In short, when they care. Twelve children were swallowed by the darkness last month. When they re-emerged into the light, they brought the rest of us with them.

21

Finding the Centre

Turning and turning in the widening gyre
The falcon cannot hear the falconer;
Things fall apart; the centre cannot hold;
Mere anarchy is loosed upon the world,
The blood-dimmed tide is loosed, and everywhere
The ceremony of innocence is drowned;
The best lack all conviction, while the worst
Are full of passionate intensity.

W. B. Yeats, 'The Second Coming'

The deep thoughts of poets, whose words can express such profound and indefinable realities, should be much lauded. It is possible to be perplexed by their words, yet simultaneously touched by them.

When the playwright Samuel Beckett was asked why his plays were difficult to understand, his explanation was that there were not enough words in the English language to express the things he was trying to say. Perhaps he had a point; there are some truths, some depths of thought, that are simply beyond words. However, I am utterly certain that all humans have the capacity, at some conscious level, to recognise the truth either with very few words or none at all. One of my favourite quotes is from Abraham Lincoln: 'You can fool some of the people all of the time, and all of the people some of the time, but you cannot fool all of the people all of the time.'

In another reflection in this book, I tried to highlight the innate solidarity in human beings that can shine through superficial everyday turmoil; Yeats, in just a few words, laments the fact that humanity is losing touch with the truth which is at its centre, at the very heart of things, the point at which all individual elements are held together in some kind of hidden cohesion. If we lose touch with that central reality, we become insulated from the central unity of human life and things become fragmented and fall apart.

Yeats sees this. The autonomous falcon is drifting further and further away and can no longer hear the falconer, the connection at the centre. Things fall apart. Turmoil and chaos are the result of it drifting so far and losing touch. The result is a dreary resignation and a loss of hope – the best lack conviction and resign themselves to powerlessness, while the worst – oppressive regimes, dictators and terrorists – are 'full of passionate intensity'.

Apply that to our present-day world of distorted passions, and perhaps the way out of the fog is for us to turn inwards and reconnect to the interior of things, both as individuals and collectively, in order to recognise our inner capacity for unity, empathy and belonging.

We are all well aware that the centre is not holding and that things are falling apart, and we have no choice but to see the only answer available to us. There are no great leaders or gurus crashing through the doors, finding the answers and making things better. The universe has gifted humanity with this amazing planet Earth to cherish in order that we may progress and flourish. It starts with you and me. Each of us is intricately tied into the universe and sharing a global responsibility. This should be challenging us and making us feel concerned and at the same time stimulated, with all of us participating in the ongoing future of the universe that gave us life? Why do we lack conviction? We're too preoccupied on the periphery and mistakenly believe we have no time to step back in order to reflect on the deep and compelling issues that confront us.

What will hold the centre is an interdependent army of people, armed with conviction and a belief in human life. A team of warriors, across continents, who are joined at the centre by a natural union of hearts and minds. As Blanche Gallagher writes in her book *Meditations with Teilhard de Chardin*: 'The more we are energetically united with others, the more our creative differences bring the planet to higher development.' Simple words, but they say everything. And never before in our history have we been more in need of hearing them.

We know the turmoil our world is in; we share Yeats's lament – the whole *world* is anguished about the state of things. What we are missing is a reassessment of the meaning, value and dignity of human existence. I love the questions Simon Conway Morris asks in his fabulous book *Life's Solution*: 'If there's a meaning and purpose to human life, why would we not want to know about it? And since we have this mysterious sense that there is, why is the question not asked?' Indeed.

Viktor E. Frankl's book *Yes to Life, in Spite of Everything* urges us to take action: 'We have to strive towards a new humanity ... Everything depends on the individual human being, regardless of how small a number of like-minded people there are ... What does life expect of me? What task is waiting for me? ... The meaning of life is waiting for us; it is the challenge of the hour ... In his or her particular area of life, every human being is irreplaceable and inimitable.'

Who, then, will volunteer? Who will be part of that small number of like-minded people discovering, re-establishing and holding the centre? It's the young who are leading the way – just witness Greta sitting on the pavement on a school strike against climate change, because what's the point of education if there's no future?

22

Turning Inwards

Indisputably, deep within ourselves, an interior appears at the heart of beings ... everything has an inside.

Teilhard de Chardin

People can live their lives largely missing a whole dimension. It's so easy to bypass it by just taking what comes and drifting through life in a sort of comfort zone, paddling in the safety of the shallows, without ever plunging into the thrills and challenges of the deep. We are risk-averse, but deep down we know that human beings are made to be part of the whole human venture, but some of them just don't know it.

From time to time, that latent spirit bursts through and reminds us of who we are and the resources available to us. There are countless examples of such resourcefulness in the face of challenge. Some years ago, a man stopped his car to help someone with a puncture, only for another driver, travelling well above the speed limit, to crash into him before driving away. Unfortunately, the Good Samaritan had to have both his legs amputated below the knee. Yet three years later,

I discovered he was taking part in a charity run, running with prosthetic blades. It's incredible how the human spirit can overcome adversity and emphatically refuse to be defeated.

Surely now, in this tumultuous world, it is time to stop underestimating ourselves and believe in ourselves? We are more than capable of reasoning a way out of chaos; we are not meant to simply ignore it. Collectively, we have the means to figure out that all turmoil is superficial. The future of our species, as we continue to evolve, must be in realising that the only possible response to chaos is collective. We need to become conscious of the potential at the heart of human existence; when every person understands their own unique and essential role as being part of the whole, we can begin to see the bigger picture.

And no, it's not difficult, and it doesn't cost anything – it's just about cultivating what's already naturally there. We all daydream, and psychologists agree how therapeutic that can be. It very easily leads to deeper thought, which begins to uncover what's truly in our minds – all we need to do is engage with and not underestimate the amazing gift of reflective consciousness that life offers. Away from the noise, away from outside influences and pressures, we *need* to know ourselves. Only then can you, as Shakespeare's Polonius advises his son Laertes in *Hamlet*, 'to thine own self be true, And it must follow, as the night the day, thou canst not then be false to any man.' These words sum up how to be an authentic human person and, in doing so, achieve self-acceptance and self-respect. This, in turn, leads to freedom: freedom from negative influences and self-doubt.

We have the privilege of being able to choose whether or not to explore the inside of things, to try to make sense of our own existence and become sensitive to the value of every human life. Imagine if every person, in order to practise the art of living, chose to spend time alone with their thoughts, in privacy and solitude, and become conscious of their own inner value. Without doubt, the world would change. Why? Here's the punchline: when I'm sure of my own inner value, the scales fall away from my eyes and I can begin to see the inner value of others. Not on the outside of things, which is where we all struggle, but on the inside, at the centre, where we are all connected.

Still not sure? Let me remind you of another great thinker, Steve Jobs, a man who changed the world in a pretty spectacular way, making it possible for everyone not just to communicate with everyone else anywhere in the world, but to access untold knowledge from something that could be held in the palm of your hand. You may have wondered where on Earth all his creative ingenuity came from. His advice to the graduating class of Stanford in 2005 explains precisely:

> Your time is limited, so don't waste it living someone else's life. Don't be trapped by dogma – which is living with the results of other people's thinking. Don't let the noise of others' opinions drown out your own inner voice. And most important, have the courage to follow your heart and intuition. They somehow already know what you truly want to become. Everything else is secondary.

23

The Process of Becoming

*That which takes place in all of us when, as we grow
up, we become aware of our family, our past and present
responsibilities, our ambitions and our loves, is nothing but
a brief recapitulation of a vaster and slower process through
which the whole human race must pass in its growth from
infancy to maturity ... but have we pondered it to the
point of realising the full intensity and extent of its truth?
It denotes the reality of a growth of humanity through and
above the growth of the individual.*

Teilhard de Chardin

In my imagination, I can see a stern Victorian father telling
his adult son to go into the world and make something of
himself. I can also imagine a parallel whereby the entire
human species (minus the stern father) may have similarly
come of age. We've made some great progress, but we need
to take on the seriously adult task of making something of
our world – but at present, we show little sign of caring
for it.

We seem powerless in the face of hunger and extreme poverty and are still engaging in such juvenile activities as terrorism, dropping bombs on innocent people and stockpiling horrendous weapons. This is *not* just a stage we are going through – history shows that the barbarian element in human life was there from the word go – but is it not now time to call time on it? Teilhard de Chardin asks us to consider the whole human species in the same way we would any individual progressing from infancy to maturity. From the moment a baby is born, it feels its way towards growth and a process of becoming adult. This involves learning, understanding, education and, most importantly, *trial and error* – learning by mistakes. I well remember, as a stroppy teenager, being told by my mother: 'Isn't it about time you grew up?' I also remember the age of twenty-one being deemed the year of adulthood, of cards and cakes emblazoned with a key, symbolising that the person was sufficiently grown-up to be trusted with the keys to the house.

Perhaps the turmoil in our present world suggests that, as a species, we have not yet reached maturity and hypothetically are not yet allowed the keys; part of the process is the realisation that as things are not what they should be, it's now time to take on the collective responsibility of delivering ourselves from the turmoil and start making the world a better place. The growth of humanity can *only* be achieved through the growth of individuals, and – as I've said before – each of us is vital to the process.

Isolationist separatism – every man for himself, every country for themselves – simply isn't working. We are not just killing each other – we're killing *our* planet. And it's not the power-obsessed despots and puffed-up leaders who will have to face that moment of doom – it will be our children's children, and generations beyond. Can we not now see writ large that there is only one way to progress further, and that is for humans to engage much more closely with each other? Not just on a personal level, but globally – nations working with other nations. We all belong to the same human family: we all live in on the same planet. The wonderful John Lennon 'imagined' all the people sharing all the world – why can't we make that a reality? Somehow, we all intuitively know that things should be different; if we think deeply about that, we may also wonder why they are not, and how it is that we seem so powerless. In terms of the analogy of our journey towards maturity, just as the adolescent has to learn that sulking in isolation never works, the way for humans to now progress further is to join forces and *'the world will be as one'*.

Naive optimism? Far from it – it is simply *adult* thinking. Maturity means starting to *seriously* believe in ourselves as a species, and not to underestimate the truth of who we are. As I said in the previous chapter, we have not yet become fully conscious of our own significance, we lack confidence and we are not yet fully aware of our potential and responsibility. How sad is it, to borrow from Tennyson, 'To rust unburnish'd, not to shine in use'.

We can come together to change the world without – and this is, perhaps, the most crucial bit – losing any of our unique identity and culture. After 'love', my second favourite four-letter word is 'team' – as we will see later, the two are strongly connected. I share the guardianship of my beloved football club, Norwich City, and consider myself privileged to have witnessed it in action over many years. Players from every nation, colour, class and creed have crossed continents to be part of our team. If each member of the team were identical, what a poor show that would be! It's the diverse and unique aspects of each team member that, when they are combined, lead to success. The human masses that are lumped together in totalitarian systems can never succeed. But unity with diversity, the essence of true democracy, is something we can strive for.

One of my favourite musicians, Pharrell Williams, once said, 'I am a slave only to my curiosity.' Fabulous. Why should we not all be slaves to our curiosity, why would we not want to know everything we can, including the mysteries of the cosmos and the big unanswered question: why humans? We are undergoing a process of *becoming* and, one day, peace and harmony will be within our reach. Another passage from Victor E. Frankl's *Man's Search For Meaning* comes to mind:

> The intensification of one's inner life … The consciousness of one's inner value … Everyone has his or her own specific vocation or mission in life; everyone must carry out a concrete assignment that demands fulfilment. Therein he cannot be replaced, nor can his life be repeated. Thus, everyone's task is unique as is his specific opportunity to implement it.

What humanity needs is not a tensionless state, but rather the striving for a worthwhile goal and a freely chosen task.

24

The Evil Trap

I enquired into the nature of evil and found no substance there.

Augustine

Evil is more of an intellectual concept than a true reality.

'Abdu'l-Bahá

People tend to believe evil is something external to them...

Carl Jung

Why is there evil in the world? This perennial question has a million and one theories, yet no definitive answers. We complain loudly and bitterly about the evil in the world, but we remain strangely indifferent and blindly accepting of it; like Tennyson's ill-fated soldiers, 'Ours is not to reason why'. Yet humans are born to reason why and to have a passion for knowledge and understanding. Tennyson wrote those words lamenting the absence of reason in the absolute absurdity of war, and reason is the major factor to consider when approaching the dreaded subject of what we call evil.

The word evil dates back to Anglo-Saxon times. If you go back further – to ancient Aramaic, Hebrew or Greek – its meaning is expressed with less intriguing words, like 'badness' or 'wrongdoing', caused by the absence of good. Once the word evil arrived on the scene, it evolved into a generic term that went beyond plain old badness and became something else: a kind of extra-terrestrial force that found its way into myths, folklore and fairy tales, before expanding into dark fiction and horror movies. Some took it further still: we have witnessed the rise of sects, cults and religions that regard evil as something outside of us that we have to overcome.

Perhaps, in our contemporary world, shaking ourselves free of myths, malevolent forces and evil eyes would be a huge step towards maturity. Instead, we should attempt to reassess what we call evil and what it actually is and – far more pertinently – what it isn't. Bad wolves, devils and demons are part of a grand cover-up, a blame game, an 'I don't know what got into me' culture. Or, to put it another way: '*Something* has to be responsible for the terrible things that happen in the world.'

The question, then, is what *is* responsible? Away from blame games, the uncomfortable answer is that it's all down to us humans. We have sole responsibility. But, and this is important, no one is born bad, and we all have a far greater capacity for good. So, to rephrase the question, what makes us bad? How do some of us become perpetrators of violence and cruelty, yet remain capable of tenderness, compassion and goodness?

The central reason for the existence of evil is a lack of knowledge about ourselves as a species, and what it is that distorts the truth and makes us vulnerable. If we don't truly know ourselves, we lack belief in who we are, in the dignity of human life and its presence in the universe. Progress is a fact: we now walk on the moon, cure fatal diseases, discover what makes black holes in space, harness the energy of the wind and the Sun and can carry the combined knowledge and communications network of the world around with us in one hand. Yet we also languish in an innocent kind of inertia and powerlessness that puts up with evil and chaos, never dreaming that if we are responsible for it then, equally, we can solve it. Lots of people are attempting this, at many levels and in many different ways, but we need a universal concerted effort. What rescues us from the dreariness of impotent resignation is a willingness to engage our instincts and understanding in order to become *alive* to the possibilities of evolution that lie ahead.

Think what that could mean: a world without hatred, violence and cruelty. Is this not what 'the process of becoming' is, aiming for a future of human flourishing and peace? A big leap forward in learning about ourselves is that we have entered a new age of psychology and the science of the mind. The renowned former Harvard professor of psychology, Roy F. Baumeister, wrote an exceptional book entitled *Evil: Inside Human Violence and Cruelty*. It is a painstaking work of research that gathers together more or less everything that is known on the subject. The book concludes: 'Evil is socially enacted and constructed. It does not reside in our genes or in our soul, but in the way we relate to other people.' In just two sentences, the challenge is set before us. The way we relate to other people. I can't help being reminded of Paul McCartney's claim in 'Let It Be' that the answer will be found when broken-hearted people in the world agree.

It is that simple. *Collectively*, we have not yet learned how to break free of the extremes of every man/woman/country for themselves and to relate effectively to one another globally. Yet however long it takes, we *are* making progress. It has been proven that the whole range of things that we call evil – inequality, wrongdoing, crime, violence, terrorism, genocide and even wars – are statistically in decline. In spite of the gloomy headlines, human progress is now a reality, which must encourage us and give us hope for the future. Only last year, Africa was declared free of wild polio and, despite almost daily news of fresh conflict, war is generally on the decline: the seventy-six years since the Second World War is the longest period of peace between the world's major powers since at least Roman times.

The world, however long it takes, is in the process of becoming a better place. And it is human beings who, in unity with diversity, can represent the front line of this evolution. As Stephen Pinker wrote in *The Better Angels of Our Nature*:

> Believe it or not – and I know that most people do not – violence has declined over long stretches of time, and today we may be living in the most peaceable era in our species' existence. The decline, to be sure, has not been smooth; it has not brought violence down to zero; and it is not guaranteed to continue. But it is an unmistakable development, visible on all scales from millennia to years, from the waging of wars to the spanking of children.

25

The Fatal Error

False and contrary to nature is the egocentric ideal of a future reserved for those who have known egotistically how to reach the extremes of 'everyone for himself'. No element can move or grow unless with, and by, means of all the others as well as itself. False and contrary to nature is the racist ideal, in which the main branch taps off all the sap of the tree for itself and rises over the death of all the others. To break through to the sun, it takes nothing less than the combined growth of the whole branching structure.

Teilhard de Chardin, *The Human Phenomenon*

I love the simplicity of Teilhard's image of humanity having to be combined in one structure in order to grow strong like a tree and break through to the sun. If overcoming all that is bad in our world depends on how we relate, or do not relate, to one another, the above is an illuminating assessment of what's wrong. However, there is hope: without some kind of cohesion of all the human elements, any form of separatist isolation or egoism is, bluntly, *'false and contrary to nature'*.

It is heady stuff and hard to take on board, but it does give an extremely coherent explanation as to why we continually live with chaos. If we are inseparable from the universe, it is hardly surprising that we are subject to its natural laws. And, while nature seems to have handed us the evolutionary reins, we are still undergoing a lengthy learning process, as we grope and feel our way towards a greater understanding of ourselves. If nature is saying no – and it *will* always have the last word – egotistical autonomy is never going to work in the long run. So, however unlikely it may seem at present, the optimistic view is that humanity will eventually achieve maturity, learning how to join forces and eliminate evil. As the great Irish statesman and philosopher Edmund Burke shrewdly observed in the eighteenth century: 'The only thing necessary for the triumph of evil is for good men to do nothing.'

The positive side of Teilhard's statement is that even in the midst of turmoil, there is something very noble and dignified in human life. Each of us has an amazing capacity for ultimate goodness; we may not be fully aware of it, but we are always on the brink of understanding. Somehow, somewhere, we know. How can *I* make a difference? Just understanding that no element can grow without all the others is a good start. In my dreams, I can see all this being part of our future education. Imagine egoism as an A-level subject! Even small children can learn how not to be egoists or racists and shown why. They should also have to learn how all of us working together is the only way to make inroads into the turmoil.

Egoism is the root of the problem. It begins with the view that, as individuals, we are alone in being responsible for our lives and that, although loosely connected, we need to be independent, in order that we can fulfil ourselves without the need of others. A small child sulkily refusing to allow a parent to fasten his shoes believes he can do it himself, but he actually can't, so eventually he will be forced to either sacrifice his desired autonomy or not go out to play. The sports psychologist Professor Damian Hughes speaks about the team being more important than the win. Egoism is an anathema to the concept of team; the 'all about me' team members are doomed in the long term, however talented they are. Success depends, first and foremost, on a team who are truly committed to one another, as is the wider team of coaches around them. To paraphrase Teilhard, 'No team can move grow or win unless with and by means of all the others.'

How simplistic that sounds – perhaps it is so simplistic that we miss it. A willingness to be humble enough to accept that will always be the way forward. In reality, in the way nature intended, there are no exceptionally amazing people who are a cut above all the rest. But there are some people who initially can't accept that, maybe because of particular circumstances in their lives. Unless they can be given some kind of reassurance or affirmation, they can feel threatened by the gifts of others and so, to overcome the insecurity and measure up, they cultivate an autonomy that can insulate them from others and blind them to the error of 'everyone for themselves'. The egoist then lives in perpetual fear of anything or anyone who may threaten to destroy what becomes a false and inflated self-image. Thus they are never wrong about anything; they need to be looked up to and highly thought of, to desire to have power over others they blindly believe to be inferior. All this helps to secure an imagined supremacy that, in the extreme, can become narcissism.

When egoism spreads, it becomes the most deadly and destructive force on our planet: racism. Racism flatters a collective egoism with the belief that there are certain privileged groups, nations, countries or cultures that are above all the rest. Racism, or in its other form fascism, is the most pernicious manifestation of what has been, and still is, wrong in our world. Unchecked, it becomes so intoxicating that egoists become blind to natural reasoning and totally immune to any kind of concern for others. In other words, they become *inhuman*.

History is littered with towering egoists such as Mussolini and Hitler, who were responsible for heinous human suffering and loss of life, but all egoism and racism is fraught with fear. What it fears most, and is intent on destroying, is unity. True democracy is, in essence, the unity of all human beings. It is not threatened by diversity but embraces it and arrives at a common-sense shared vision of how we can live in a world of peaceful cooperation.

Create division and you achieve your aim to weaken others and preserve your own elitist status. The only thing necessary for humanity to triumph over egoism is for good people to do *something*, and the best thing they can do is join forces. And why on earth not? We already share culture, ingenuity and invention: one nation invents football while another discovers the theory of relativity. How did we get to eat pizza, drink Rioja, gaze at paintings by Picasso and listen to Beethoven? We should be celebrating what we belong to and are part of: a dazzlingly diverse, inventive and ingenious world community.

We have come a very long way: there is almost no slavery, and most nations have instituted civil rights. But the injustice of racism has not yet been fully banished, and the racist elements in our society are attempting a resurgence. Perhaps (and we have to hope this is true) it's a sort of last gasp because the end is in sight; there is no place for racism in a converging world of mass communication and mass migration, with nations joining forces. Teilhard felt that it would be easier to stop the world turning than to stop it from converging. Now that every subject under the sun – science, medicine, space exploration – is being furthered by joint effort, no isolated 'great nation' is changing the world and all nations are combining their ingenuity, so there is cause for optimism. It's pessimism that makes the headlines, but maybe the days of demagogues and inflated egos are numbered. If we consider that nature's way means that, as Teilhard said, 'no element can move or grow unless with and by the means of all the others', then surely, thankfully, we are seeing humanity awakening to all kinds of possibilities, including learning how to call time on the fatal errors of egoism and racism. The following quote from Horace's *Epistles* feels appropriate here:

> You may drive out Nature with a pitchfork,
> But she will ever hurry back to triumph
> In stealth over your foolish contempt.

PART THREE

The Human is the Solution

26

The Solution

The human being can have no hope of an evolutionary future except in association with all the rest ... and not to see it we have to close our eyes.

Teilhard de Chardin, *The Human Phenomenon*

So, eyes wide open for this one, yet it would seem that, as we near the end of the first quarter of the twenty-first century, we are blindly sleepwalking into one catastrophe after another. Not least the indifference from some nations and world leaders to the extreme gravity of climate change, the risks posed to the environment and the resulting deadly Covid-19 pandemic. Biodiversity acts as a buffer to the spread of disease – as it decreases, we are more vulnerable to further pandemics.

There is no doubting how far we have advanced as a species, so how come we have not yet managed to combine our cumulative genius to eradicate these appalling threats to our future, or to learn the lessons of the past? Instead, humans are still behaving like barbarians.

There are currently, according to Amnesty International, a million people being detained in something similar to concentration camps. The BBC programme *Outside Source* showed horrific footage of what those people are suffering. So it has come full circle – yet another racist attempt to separate a whole community from the rest while subjecting them to untold cruelty. We also saw on our TV screens how the Rohingya community of Myanmar were killed, tortured and driven out of their country, while everything they owned was burned to the ground. There are now millions of homeless refugees throughout the planet fleeing violence and life-threatening situations, while millions more people are refusing to offer help and shelter. In my country, we currently have a chronic shortage of lorry drivers for deliveries, a collapsing hospitality industry with no staff, a shortage of health workers – the list goes on. What do we do? We offer our neighbours in France lashings of money to stop refugees and potential workers entering our country, who could in time do all those things. There is, however, hope on the horizon, as young, energised people are seeing and refusing to accept how things are. Witness Greta Thunberg and Marcus Rashford, who as role models are inspiring millions of other young people. I'm hopeful that this momentum could be the beginning of a new generation with get-up-and-go minds and hearts who are not afraid to attempt to change the world. It's hard to think that anyone would not want that, but first we have to see in sharp focus the horrendous atrocities our species is responsible for.

Sometimes there are specific moments when you have what's called an epiphany, when you come face to face with how things really are. It happened to me not so long ago when I took some trainees from our football youth academy to visit the magnificent Sainsbury Centre for Visual Arts at the University of East Anglia. Among the paintings by Degas, Francis Bacon, Picasso and many other diverse and awesome works of art, we came across one painting that made a deep impression on us all. It was a portrait of an old man with a knowing but wistfully sad gaze. The curator explained that it was a self-portrait by a Slovenian artist called Zoran Music, a supremely gifted artist, who had been incarcerated at Dachau concentration camp. There, he witnessed thousands of people being brutally treated, before slowly and painfully starving to death. Zoran managed to survive the camp and became a much-acclaimed artist, but he was continually haunted not just by his experience, but by the realisation that the words 'it could never happen again' were a delusion. Twenty-five years after surviving the horrors of the camp, he concluded that nothing had changed, so felt compelled to record the horror of what he had witnessed in a extensive collection of agonising paintings entitled *We Are Not the Last.*

Like other survivors, Music was intent on reminding people that they must *never* forget. The paintings show harrowing ghostly images of endless corpses, a gruelling and powerful witness to the extreme human brutality. Yet he also saw something deeply spiritual in the heaps of dried-out, twisted corpses: the unseen beauty and true essence of humanity somehow transcended what the Nazis had attempted to obliterate. Within the atrocity, and in spite of it, he saw something in humanity that is beyond the reach of egoist racism. For me, his moving self-portrait was a shocking and bleak reminder that everything *is still the same* and that all those who were victims of such atrocities were certainly not the last.

It is easy to feel powerless when faced with this reality, but we have the solution in front of our eyes – as long as we keep them open. All it involves is people associating with one another much more closely; all people, from all nations, learning how to be what they truly are. The poet John Donne understood this 400 years ago, when he wrote: 'No man is an island entire of itself … every man … is a part of the main … any man's death diminishes me'.

Teilhard talks about the 'grandeur of the human mission', and what I think he means seems very plausible. Here we are, existing on this beautiful planet with everything we could possibly need for enriched meaningful lives, and the whole point is to make a success of it and ensure that all life on Earth progresses. We all know there's no such thing as a free lunch – there's cost, labour and continued effort. But what price human flourishing and peace on Earth? What other possible mission could we have – and yes, it is a very grand and challenging concept. Churchill, when facing a crisis, wanted the population 'to discover a spirit they may not know they had'. The same goes for now. To see and believe in our true selves, and a spirit of unity and goodness that exists, beyond the terror and the chaos, so that we can say what Zoran Music was unable to: everything is *not* the same. The astronaut Ron Garan summed this up perfectly:

> For me it was an epiphany in slow motion. It's a profound sense of empathy, a profound sense of community and a willingness to forego immediate gratification and take a more multi-generational outlook on progress … From space, the planet is a constantly changing masterpiece and the sheer beauty is absolutely breathtaking … But another thing that hit me was a

sobering contradiction between the beauty of our planet and the unfortunate realities of life on our planet. It filled me with a sense of injustice. It infuriated me.

You can be sat up there in orbit thinking about this contradiction and then realise you're sitting on the answers. The answer is that humans – when they set aside their differences and work together – can do anything.

27

There's Only One *You*

Exclusively, solely, entirely, uniquely, wholly you!
With help from a thesaurus

The emphasis this time round is on *you* – as you may have gathered! This is because only one by one can humans commit to uniting with one another. To put it another way, recognising the unseen cohesion between us is the only way to find solutions in a disaffected world. I know it doesn't sound credible – one humorous interpretation suggested that persuading humans to unite would be like trying to herd cats! But after many years of study and observation, I am convinced that every human has an innate capacity to recognise truth. First, however, we need to *want* truth. We are free to evade it, deny it or be selective with it, but for those who seek it, the truth will find that it always resonates at a deeper level.

Socrates said that it takes courage to conquer not others, but yourself, to cultivate a desire to know and become who you truly are. There is a better part of us that can stay hidden in the midst of the world's turmoil. When the dying young woman on page 4 finally recognised the truth of her existence, it was beyond her wildest dreams.

Why is it so many of us never realise that? Because we're told otherwise. Whoever came up with the phrase 'blinded by science' had a point: many scientists believe that, on a cosmic scale, humans are some kind of chance happening, without meaning and purpose. What silence and reflection shows is this is not the case. We must dare to first believe in ourselves, and then what follows is a belief in the coming together of humanity, and the enormous possibilities that open up ahead. Once we are free of pettiness, small-mindedness, of being told what to think and believe, we are able to see how to *give* ourselves and make a difference, a personal contribution to solving the world's problems. If everyone could buy into first knowing themselves, this would quickly become a *shared vision* of unity – common sense, a common task and a common mission.

One of history's great thinkers, Blaise Pascal, summed it up brilliantly: 'All the troubles of life come upon us because we refuse to sit quietly for a while each day in our rooms.' The happy simplicity of what he is saying is: it's not a big deal. Yet if enough of us were to buy into it, the outcome could be the biggest deal ever. If, through collective reflection, we are able to see 'the troubles of life' more clearly, we then begin to see the solutions. What was once incomprehensible becomes not only possible, but logical and even obvious.

Remember the famous First World War poster of Lord Kitchener pointing his finger and the caption: 'Your Country Needs You'? Hundreds of thousands of young people willingly responded, wanting to help, to buy into a collective effort with a passion and a purpose which could mean sacrificing their lives for their country. One hundred years on, that same poster should be posted everywhere and changed to read: 'Your Planet Needs You!'

We can never overestimate the power of the human spirit. But only each one of us in union with the rest can make up a whole, and that in time is the one and only thing that can provide solutions.

28

Socialisation

In every organised whole, the parts perfect themselves and fulfil themselves. It is a mistake to confuse individuality with personality. To be fully ourselves it is in the direction of convergence with all the rest that we must advance – towards the 'other.' The peak of ourselves, the acme of our originality, is not in our individuality but in our person; and according to the evolutionary structure of the world, we can only find our person by uniting together. Socialisation means, not the end, but rather the beginning of the Era of Person.

Teilhard de Chardin, *The Human Phenomenon*

The above quote is a bold and challenging statement. Teilhard was certainly a century ahead of his time, but what he's saying is becoming more and more plausible and relevant. Now in the twenty-first century, convergence is being mapped out by science, but we are not yet fully awake to how this could be the beginning of a new era. I have already written about how, on the surface, humans appear to oppose each other at every level, hence the conflict and disorder. Yet we can't deny the illuminative flashes of unity between us, particularly in times of crisis. Very early in the coronavirus pandemic, people began to take more notice of one another and care about each other – and that, in turn, made them feel good about *themselves*. It was a moment in time when everyone had the desire, if not the means, to leap up and do anything they could to help. It seems that in deep anxiety, our hidden connectedness naturally surfaces, as we are reminded of what we truly are, and instantly adapt to it.

Human beings belong to one another as part of a whole; however long it takes, maybe centuries, we are entering a process of socialisation and becoming an *organised* whole. This basic premise of individuals being crucial in the functioning of the whole is essential for the future of the planet. *There are no alternatives* – conflict isn't working. As the human species matures, the evidence of this is starting to come more into focus. What we learned from the last century, for instance, is that Marxism failed by trying to lump everyone together in one supposedly equal mass, which removed individual identity from people, along with their freedom and democracy. If only we could fully realise what the power of global unity could achieve, or what optimists like me would say *will* be achieved: the end of demagogues and military regimes, and the latest attempt at massing people together under the flag of so-called populism will be similarly doomed. In the end, whatever name you give it, it is all the same thing: the manipulation of the masses by the few. In a new enlightened age of convergence, this will come to an end. A time will come when it will be the coalescing masses that determine the future, and populism will join communism and fascism in being consigned to history.

Focusing on the future and on the role of individuals, one of Teilhard's most quoted phrases is: 'true union differentiates ... a convergent universe with the power to extend the individual fibres that compose it without being lost in the whole – each element achieves uniqueness and completeness ... Life has an objective but can only be attained by all drawing together more closely in every sense – individually, socially, nationally and racially.' What a dream! Instead of losing our identity when we join forces with others, the opposite happens: we become more ourselves and reach the pinnacle of our 'uniqueness and completeness'. One person's talent complements another person's talent and each person can shine more brightly, enhanced by the others.

Imagine every living person reaching their very best by consciously joining forces with all the rest. Person to person, nation to nation, all contributing to a process of unity. No egoism, no deluded isolationists, no going it alone, no superior elites or repressive regimes, no dictators, no left or right – extreme or otherwise. Because I know who I am, and you know who you are – everyone is walking tall, no need to try to be different because we will all know we are different, yet at the same time united in a common purpose: changing – or should I say, given our current circumstances – *saving* the world.

And without greed, resentment and all the rest, guess what? Suddenly there *is* enough food to feed the world, while united efforts *can* sort out climate change, disease and other grave challenges, because everyone wants the same thing. Best of all, the economy turns out not to be the mainstay of our existence at the expense of everything else; unity without conflict can achieve a healthy climate, with all nations flourishing and sharing the world's resources. All of a sudden, the economy is thriving as well!

What I am imagining may turn out not to be naive optimism, but part of a universal strategy that is awaiting us, a concession to what nature intended all along: *all humans being equal.*

Everything I am trying to say here can be simplified to one glorious sentence. It was coined by an American author called Ken Blanchard, who lectures all over the world on leadership in business: *None of us is as smart as all of us.* When I first became the director of Norwich City Football Club twenty-five years ago, I commissioned an artist to paint a picture with the large letters NCFC, with each letter illustrating board directors, then staff, then footballers and lastly supporters, with the caption 'None of us is as smart as all of us'. It now hangs in the club reception. So I have lived with those words over many years knowing how profound they are, in spite of their simplicity. The truth is that *'none of us is as smart as all of us.'* And this should be the rallying cry for a world facing crisis.

29

Team World

The human brain, it seems, is designed to both work hard to produce a sense of coherence and meaning and then to respond positively to this sense when it arises. This is why investing time in painting the bigger picture is so essential to the creation of a high-performing culture.

The emerging consensus is that, from an evolutionary point of view, the drive for contextualisation and coherence is an essential tool for dealing with a complex and bewildering environment. Seeking meaning through a positive feeling of purpose also creates a sense of dissatisfaction with the status quo, which in turn leads us to break new ground and make something more of ourselves and the world.

Damian Hughes, *The Barcelona Way:*
How to Create A High-Performance Culture

Damian Hughes is an eminent psychology professor, whose work has led to him being a consultant to leading professionals in sport and business around the world. His book *The Barcelona Way* is, for me, unique in the way that it marries the advances of psychology with the knowledge and the experience of leading figures in sport. It paints a vivid picture of the enormous potential of *collective* human endeavour, not just in sport but in life. I'm now convinced that sport can provide a template for a high-performing culture in all areas of daily life, and it's impossible to paint a bigger picture than that!

I know I've mentioned it before, but the concept of team has so much to teach us. First, there is no complexity to navigate, it is grounded in simplicity but also in learning, as everyone has to learn how to be a team member. So coaching for beginners starts with learning about behaviour. First and foremost, the coach has to teach young athletes how to develop themselves by focusing on others, because that's what makes them better people; being late is being selfish, as is not clearing away the coffee cups and not acknowledging, engaging with or caring for other people. Team prioritises cohesion with others. As Damian puts it, 'we must try to develop ourselves, by at the same time developing a social glue'. That's probably the best description of team I've yet heard. Clearly, what's missing in our disaffected world is a rather large amount of social glue!

The bigger picture begins and ends with behaviour. One coach said: 'Talent will get you through the door of the dressing-room, but only behaviour will keep you there.' Damian says there are three key elements in teamwork:

- Humility, which he says is the bedrock of learning.
- Hard work.
- Realising that the team is more important than winning, which is logical, since you have to be a close-knit team in order to win.

All this finds parallels in life: having meaning and a positive purpose, not just putting up with the status quo but wanting to break new ground and make something of ourselves. Sport and life are one and the same. If it were up to me, I would make Damian Hughes minister of education and life coaching. Just imagine if we all had lessons in how to behave. Picnic rubbish wouldn't be left in the countryside or on the beach. There would be no skipping queues or parking in disabled bays, and everyone would care for others. And then we would find that a minor miracle occurs. You are being cared for because you belong to a team; just keep imagining it over and over. *Team World.*

Every team member is vital to the others, and this is how union really does differentiate. I can't do what you do – but your support in what I do enables me to become the best I can be, and vice versa. If any member of the team wants to be elevated and more important than the others, they can no longer play a part. Certain football managers have been bold enough to replace big-name, talented players with those who are less gifted but understand the behavioural rules and make a better contribution to the team. What is to be achieved can only be achieved by all; unity rules, unleashing an unawakened energy, a fundamental energy that all other energies merely serve. Then that combined energy unleashes its power. The power of collaborative human brains and human effort can *achieve anything.*

To build a team, hope and optimism are key. When Barack Obama, in his victory speech following the 2008 presidential election, declared 'Yes we can!', he was encouraging the American people to see a bigger picture ahead for their nation, but back then, not enough people were *personally* committed to joining him in his vision. In order to become Team World, we have to realise that only when *all* of us are willing to buy into a shared vision can it happen. Thus the whole concept of what we call 'top-down' hierarchies, in terms of the future organisation of the planet, has become totally outdated and about as far away from team as you can get.

One of the fiercest divisions of all is nationalism versus globalism. Nationalism looks increasingly juvenile, since the world is now so connected and global; the idea of nations going it alone and being obsessed with their own exclusive national sovereignty is archaic.

Teilhard, almost a century ago, said: 'The age of nations is past'. Yet, as with each of us individually, every nation has its own character, ethos and culture that is important to the rest. It is not meant to be forfeited, but preserved and enriched with the help and support of the rest, as they in turn receive the same.

Just over half a century ago, in America, US president John F. Kennedy saw all this and gave a prophetic address on Independence Day in 1962. He spoke of the origins of the American Declaration of Independence and added his own vision of the future, which he outlined as 'interdependence'. He mentioned the establishment in 1957 of the European Economic Community – countries forming a union with one another in order to work together – and spoke compellingly: 'If there is a single issue in the world which divides the world, it is independence.' He said that the American constitution was designed to 'encourage both differences and dissent' and that 'it stressed not independence but interdependence, not the individual liberty of one but the indivisible liberty of all.' He went on to say, 'a great new effort for interdependence is transforming the world about us … to find freedom in diversity and, in unity, strength … Acting on our own, by

ourselves, we cannot establish justice throughout the world
… But joined with other free nations, we can do all this and
more. We can assist the developing nations to throw off the
yoke of poverty. We can balance our worldwide trade and
payments at the highest possible level of growth.'

Finally, Kennedy quoted Abraham Lincoln's promise of
'not only liberty to the people of this country but hope to
the world … Hope that in due time, the weight should be
lifted from the shoulders of all men and that all should have
an equal chance.'

If ever there was a prophetic vision of a movement towards
'Team World', that was it. It was not, alas, achievable in his
very short time in office, but the seeds were sown. Global
thinking is on the rise and will continue to gestate, and if
our younger and future generations buy into the idea, we are
guaranteed to break new ground and make something more
of ourselves and the world. And who knows – perhaps I can
dare to dream that 'Team World United' could turn up on a
T-shirt, hopefully sometime soon.

30

Workers of the World

Humanity is beginning to understand that we are not and cannot be mere onlookers in the immensity of evolution. We are now seeing that we have a collective work to carry through ... the world has a future and it is we who are building that future ... I would show those whose lives are dull and drab the limitless horizons opening out to humble and hidden efforts ... make life more passionately interesting even in the most common place and the most tedious setting.

Teilhard de Chardin

What is being said above is pivotal, and needs to be thought about over a period of time – perhaps every day. Almost a century after those words were written, we are still only on the brink when it comes to understanding their implications. Teilhard uses another phrase, 'the world is still under construction', which, for me, really puts it in context. In my mind, I imagine the Earth covered with scaffolding, with everyone beavering away to get it finished. And that, in truth, is where we are, except the building is in danger of collapsing and needs far more labourers to join the effort.

We are the most privileged species. Having been gifted an amazingly exquisite planet, we are tasked with caring for it and making something of it. What a mission – to have a responsibility and an equally valued part to play in achieving success and securing Earth's future. That's hard to grasp in a world of dissent and chaos, which is precisely the problem. Until, that is, we understand that everyone's personal effort is required in building the Earth, in order to flourish, progress and ultimately live in peace and harmony. It's not rocket science – it's massively more significant.

We have already given thought to each of us being our own project and knowing ourselves. Call that 'phase one'. 'Phase two' is that once that happens we are set free from misconceptions and anxieties about ourselves and can be free to become a worker for 'Project World', a grander human mission that gives new meaning and purpose to our lives. Human life is destined to succeed. Its mission is to mature, advance and progress. It involves labour and toil, trial and error, dedication, effort and hardship. What price peace and harmony on Earth, and ultimate joy and celebration? Ask the athlete clutching the medal or lifting the cup. Job done. Work completed.

The psychiatrist Viktor Frankl, having spent time in a concentration camp and then over many years dealt with thousands of patients with mental issues, concluded that most of them were not actually suffering from mental health problems, but simply lacking meaning and purpose, which he said is the primary motivation in a person's life. He mentioned a statistical survey of 7,948 students from forty-eight colleges: 16 per cent said their primary goal was making money, while 78 per cent said their first goal was 'finding a purpose and meaning to my life'. Frankl went on to say that mental patients can lack awareness of a deeper meaning that is worth living for; they are haunted by the experience of an inner emptiness – what he called an 'existential vacuum'. Right now, I feel the vast increase in mental health issues and the lack of resources to deal with it is caused by exactly that – a lack of meaning within the chaos of our fractured world. Both Frankl and Teilhard refer to boredom as the number one human enemy, and it's on the increase due to automation, more time on our hands and increasing unemployment. The vacuum then becomes depression, aggression, addiction or worse, suicide. Our confused society is in need of healing.

It is a bold statement, but if we could all merge and be part of a vital and dynamic workforce to build the Earth, to care for it and ensure it has a future, could there be any greater mission or greater meaning or greater purpose under the sun? And what young person today would not want that? Healing sickness, eliminating disease, encouraging biodiversity and helping to sustain all forms of life and species. Healing the land and the seas that we are currently decimating. Even the most humble efforts, which we have seen in the Covid-19 pandemic, have shown people everywhere giving support and *working* for a greater cause.

I more than understand the sceptics: how on earth are we to outwit the high, the mighty and powerful, whose ignorance (albeit sometimes unintentional) is mostly responsible for our demise? The answer is in humble efforts in the most everyday, tedious settings. Witness the frail-looking fifteen-year-old Greta Thunberg. All she did was sit on a pavement outside the Swedish parliament every Friday with a notice that said 'school strike for climate change'. What could be a more

humble effort than that? We all know what happened next –
something she couldn't have dreamed of. People caught on
and it went viral around the world, inspiring other children,
who simultaneously joined Friday school strikes. As one
magazine pointed out, it was the world's children who were
informing their parents of the gravity of the situation. They
became connected globally, and the campaign led to similar
protests about American gun laws and other causes. A recent
BBC documentary calculated that over seven million young
people came out in force, giving us a small example of what
a 'social explosion' could achieve. Greta was invited to speak
at world climate summits and to meet world leaders. For
me, the most fascinating part in a documentary about her
was watching the uninterested audience of powerful leaders.
Yet the media frenzy around Greta meant that, in spite of
them, her message *was* heard around the world and inspired
millions who are now joining the call for urgent change. Her
message: 'I want you to panic ... and then I want you to act
as if your house was on fire.'

The point to stress here is that initially Greta offered all
she could: a humble gesture of sitting on a pavement. Yet
that tiny little spark from a child caring about the world and
the future of her own generation caught alight, spread like
fire and inspired young people everywhere. That's exactly it –
young people uniting to change the world and understanding
Teilhard's even bolder and much more stark words: '*Unite or
perish!*'

We can't be mere onlookers; the world has a future and
we have to build it, however humble our efforts, however
tedious our surroundings. We have each to offer something –
anything – because human life does have a meaning and a
purpose. That is what, in the end, makes it so 'passionately

interesting'. The poem 'If I Can Stop One Heart from Breaking' by Emily Dickinson sums up the message very nicely:

If I can stop one heart from breaking,
I shall not live in vain;
If I can ease one life the aching,
Or cool one pain,
Or help one fainting robin
Unto his nest again,
I shall not live in vain.

31

Covid-19: A Call to Arms

*We may have been taught humility. We have realised there
are people who are willing to sacrifice their lives to save us;
people we don't know are willing to do that. These are very
amazing things to learn. And I think that, when things
start to go back, it'll never go back to what it was.*

Michael Craig-Martin

Just a few words, but don't they speak loudly?

When I began this project, I was not under any illusions.
I knew from day one that it was going to be a tough and
lengthy task that might not work. Fast forward four years,
and what I was not at all expecting was that one subject I felt
quite determined about, the hidden goodness and unity in
humans, would suddenly leap out of hiding and become
an unquestionable, enormous and visible reality: a bright
light beaming out in the midst of such a dark and menacing
situation.

The world was suddenly, and almost without warning,
undergoing immense suffering, as the unfettered spread

of Covid-19 moved silently and swiftly across continents. Overwhelmed medical workers, unimaginable daily death tolls and relatives cut off from loved ones who lay dying. And grieving families torn apart by lockdown and barred from attending the funerals.

Yet amidst confusion, lack of information and disorganisation, the ever-beating heart and energising spirit of humanity changed gear, as people joined forces. Health workers at all levels, without thinking what the cost might be, gave and risked themselves, with many losing their own lives trying to save others. What the deadly virus could not suppress was the value of what happens when humans simply and swiftly revert to type. It seemed that, all the while, an energised, unified community had been waiting to emerge.

People in lockdown suddenly understood that they were equal members of a caring community. The elderly and frail suddenly became the focus of untold care and attention. The willingness of anyone and everyone doing anything they could to help was breathtaking. The entire nation engaged in delivering food parcels, meals, stitching medical scrubs and inventing ways to make up the shortage of visors and masks. People contacted strangers to check if they needed anything. I even heard of one lady who baked scones for the dustmen in gratitude, simply because they turned up. Everyone seemed to be baking something for those in need, so much so that flour mills were forced to organise night shifts to cope with the demand. For me personally, it was wonderful to receive so many appreciative messages for the revived recipes that we had all forgotten.

The internet buzzed with musicians, exercise lessons and poets. A never-ending stream of thoughtful enterprise was supplied to the millions who could not leave their homes, an eruption of creativity we simply marvelled at. And the most important element in the midst of such deep anxiety was *so* much brilliant and entertaining humour, as all those wonderful little films buzzed around on the internet!

During the first lockdown, in our empty football stadium, one office was buzzing, as players, staff and board directors telephoned every single season ticket-holder over the age of sixty to see if they were okay or needed anything. And every one of us who took part felt exhilarated by the responses and conversations we had, not to mention the humour: 'Hello this is your goalkeeper – I just want to know if you're okay.' At the same time, every health centre, care home and medical establishment in Norfolk received a football shirt signed by the Norwich City team and an 'Ultimate Carrot Cake' baked by our amazing chefs – thanks also to our kit team, who went on a delivery marathon. What came over loud and clear was that all those who gave their time felt as if *they* were on the receiving end. And at the same time, the entire nation was similarly engaged, giving their time to care for those in need and feeling uplifted by it.

The hero and perhaps the embodiment of it all was Captain Tom, a hundred-year-old veteran walking a marathon in his back garden with the help of a Zimmer frame, proving that everyone, whatever their age, could make a contribution. He had hoped to raise up to two thousand pounds, yet the generous response of people everywhere *also* wanting to help raised an unprecedented £32 million for the NHS. An interview with Tom's daughter revealed something very telling: throughout it all, he had begun to look younger. How many other people found that being involved and making a contribution, engaging with others and helping to make a difference, somehow enlivened their lives?

The other beacon of light that shone brightly in the darkest days of that first lockdown was the 'Clap for Carers'. A Dutch woman living in London had the amazing idea that each Thursday at 8pm, everyone would stand at their doors and windows and simultaneously clap to thank the brave health workers and those working at the frontline of the crisis. It was a very moving spectacle, and it seemed like the whole nation joined in. Children painted rainbows of hope to display in their windows, while parents banged pots and pans to show support. Clare Fallon, North of England Correspondent for Channel 4 News, watched as the entire length of an urban street was filmed clapping and cheering. When the noise died down, she turned to the camera and, in what was, for me, a precious moment that could never be recaptured, spoke from the heart: 'They are not just clapping in gratitude but a moment of unity.' How profound is that? Everyone knows it and feels it, even if we can't quite put it into words.

What struck people, over and over, was that being forced to stand back from the pressures of modern life gave them not just time to think and reflect, but an increased awareness of how beneficial having the time and space just to think could be. Also, while technology played a major role in connecting everyone, the realisation emerged that it could never replace the loss of physical human contact, something we may have taken for granted. A gentle slap on the back, a handshake, hugs and kisses, all absent against the sad eeriness and emptiness of locked doors and deserted high streets – underlining just how much people need each other and that engaging across distances can't replace times of close proximity and just being present with one another. The historian Mary Beard amusingly noted how often she had cursed crowded commuter trains that were frequently late, yet confined at home, she would have given anything to be on one. We realised during lockdown that however much other people irritate the hell out of us, the reality is that we value living alongside one another; our appreciation of that definitely went up a notch during lockdown.

What we have witnessed in the Covid-19 pandemic is that when humans become what they are naturally – a community – they reach the peak of their powers. As Michael Craig-Martin said, 'It'll never go back to what it was.'

What we have seen in one another during this catastrophe should make us feel proud. Could it be a tragedy that is also an opportunity? I admit to discovering in lockdown that I have previously taken things, and especially people, so much for granted. I have discovered that I really love our football supporters – in spite of the tiny minority of whingers. Not having them around, and the sad ghostliness of an empty stadium, feels like a tragedy in itself. On the positive side, I read a wonderful book called *The 5AM Club* and was inspired to rise at the said time and therefore not just be present at this amazing daily event we call 'the dawn', but actually sit still with nothing to do but watch it happen. There is something magical about the first light breaking through the darkness; words are inadequate, so all I can do is highly recommend it as a therapy. It's free and requires no effort (well, apart from getting out of bed), but it speaks volumes. What if the light didn't come? It's something we just take for granted, but slowly but surely, darkness is always superseded by light. Perhaps this is something to cling to and be sure of in the dark moments of the Covid-19 pandemic.

32

Covid-19: Some Reasons For Optimism

Covid-19 has revealed the mortal weaknesses of our nations. The economic costs – collapsed businesses, rising unemployment, declining growth – will threaten the future of an entire generation for decades to come. The vigilant state and society will become the new normal. We must embrace it. The threat this pandemic posed will emphasise the importance of protecting and strengthening the health of civilisations as well as communities – what one may call our planetary health.

Richard Horton, *The Covid-19 Catastrophe*

It doesn't need an inordinate amount of thought to figure out that *global* scientific teamwork and a *united* action on the gravity of climate change may have prevented Covid-19 from existing. The hundreds of thousands of people who have died could still be living with their families and communities, with so much suffering avoided. Time, in the light of this sudden and unparalleled catastrophe, to stand back and seriously contemplate its implications. It is now imperative that we consider how to deal with the extremely grave dangers threatening not just parts of the world, but its entire population.

As if we hadn't noticed, we live in an age of high-speed jets that can transport the particles that cause pandemics and deposit them anywhere within hours, while at the same time delivering poisonous fumes into the atmosphere. We could have acted immediately and grounded some of those planes, but most countries didn't. In the light of our extreme vulnerability, it would seem that our current way of life on planet Earth is in need of an urgent rethink. A new age, with new threats, demands new ingenuity and creative, joined-up thinking. This in no way denigrates past efforts and achievements, but we are compelled by present circumstances to seriously rethink how best to safeguard our future.

Could the deadly virus be a wake-up call? Or nature, perhaps, putting down a marker for those unruly tenants occupying planet Earth? What it has underlined is the urgent need for *change*. Our world – and I emphasise *our* because it belongs to all of us – is in dire need of different organisation and management. We have seen that a small group of what we call 'world leaders' are no longer appropriate or adequate for the age we live in. The present system of governance, in which the majority of the population are unable to act on their own behalf, has become precarious. To have to mutely stand aside and allow leaders, figureheads, dictators and such, to act – or *not* to act – on our behalf is not just dangerous but totally unacceptable. So often, world-affecting decisions are being made, not for the wellbeing of the people, but for various self-serving agendas. Some leaders are very good, some are better than others and some are very much worse.

The age of top-down leadership is passing, and what we now falsely call democracy is not. We urgently need to remind ourselves of the true meaning of that contaminated word. Governing thanks to a majority of votes from a misled, lied-to, manipulated population is *not* democracy. From the Greek word 'demokratia', the *Collins English Dictionary* has four interpretations: 'the practice of social equality', 'a social condition of classlessness', 'the practice or spirit of social equality' and, my own favourite, 'government by the *people*'. Demos is Greek for 'the people' and kratia is 'rule', so my reading would be that true democracy is a socially classless, equal society, in which the people rule. This poses the question of how to make that happen. How can an entire population join forces, cooperate and become an interdependent force that can overcome the dangers we are now facing?

It simply has to happen; the world *has* to move on. Thanks to technology, the planet is well-connected and networked, so now is the perfect time for us to step out of the Middle Ages and concede that the age of disparate sovereign nations acting only on their own behalf and people being 'lions led by donkeys', is coming to a close. We have seen demonstrated with clarity that this is perilous, dangerous and way behind the times. How many lives could have been saved if Donald Trump had not – in the middle of the Covid-19 pandemic – cut contributions to the World Health Organisation, an act which Horton describes as a 'crime against humanity'? Surely that would not have been the choice of the American people? We are now in an age of convergence, and Covid-19 has starkly illuminated how much we need to embrace that. Only the vigilance of *all of us in unison* can protect the planet and make us the guardians of the future.

It is frightening how the world can become unhinged, disconnected and dangerously threatened, in the midst of confusion, lack of information and disorganisation. The unfolding story of the deadly virus, right from its inception, has much to teach us about failed, fudged leadership. Rumours and counter-rumours, cover-ups, denials and mixed messages buzzed across the airwaves. There *had* been pandemics before, yet the state of unpreparedness was catastrophic. The UK, back in 2016, had sensibly commissioned Public Health England to simulate a pandemic, called Exercise Cygnus, which showed how unprepared we were and listed all sorts of recommendations. However, these recommendations remained unpublished and forgotten for the feeble reason that they might have made people panic; what a small price that would have been.

Interestingly, after about three months of Covid-19 confusion, Channel 4 showed an enlightening documentary called *The Country that Beat the Virus: What Can Britain Learn?* At last we were able to see how another country could calmly and positively confront the pandemic. South Korea (bearing in mind its proximity to China and Taiwan) had the advantage of already being prepared, having learned lessons from previous pandemics. The South Koreans took on Covid-19 with a speed and organisation that was breathtaking to watch. Infrared scanners at airports could spot anyone who had a temperature. Twenty biotech laboratories were immediately contacted and four came up with test kits, which were then passed on to a further forty-six labs; testing was up and running in just one week, at the same time the World Health Organisation was exhorting all nations to 'test, test, test'. The Korean policy was to test, contain and then trace. Simultaneously, a mobile phone app was developed that could eventually trace people who had been in contact with those with symptoms in ten minutes. What the programme did not reveal, but which perhaps explains their swift and remarkable reaction, is that according to Terence Kealey, a lecturer in clinical biochemistry at the Cato Institute in Washington, South Korea spends twice as much as the UK on scientific research, putting it before commercial innovations. So it was ready.

Imagine living in a world of truly united nations, concerned only with the wellbeing of the planet and the flourishing of life. Scientific investment would be high on the agenda, with a shared financial commitment and a combined research effort into how to deal with the grave threat of climate change and prevent the harmful viruses linked to it. Can we not see the logic in this? Collectively, human beings have the ingenuity needed to flourish and progress, but how much of that is discounted, suppressed and going to waste? Instead, we rely on a disparate handful of people at the top to make all the decisions. How much human enterprise and progress is denied in this way, and how much illness, death, poverty and inequality is caused?

We have some brave, talented and caring politicians, but today's politics, far from allowing them to join forces and serve the nations they represent, means that they are stuck in a groove of fading, divided political parties that are well past their sell-by date. The present political system isn't working; it actually promotes division and eclipses unity. So let's be adult and move beyond left-wing and right-wing, with the shadowy extremists that lurk in the wings. Party politics is so *not now*. What *is* now is a new version of politics, with shared, collaborative leadership that answers to the people.

I, along with two million other people, had a glimpse of this in action, long before Covid-19, on a Brexit protest march. The joy of uniting on a sunny day and being among families, children, dogs and politicians of all persuasions was refreshing and energising. At the end, I was very near to the platform where six MPs from different political parties stood side by side. As each one spoke, I saw a little cameo of what I have attempted to explain here. Politicians, of one mind with the people, sharing the same passion and the same vision. We did not achieve our objective, but it was exhilarating to be present and experience what was a profound moment of unity. Though our cause turned out not to be the will of the majority, I nonetheless had an overwhelming feeling that this kind of engagement is how things are meant to be.

It will take a new generation of innovators to rework the present systems and find ways for nations to work in unison. If the present systems were good, and the world and the human race was flourishing, it would be fair enough, but the pandemic has exposed weaknesses, mismanagement and unacceptable chaos. Each one of us now needs to buy into the bigger picture and have a hand in creating a united world. I have said before that unity does not mean a loss of identity and culture; all nations are enriched by the identity and culture of others. There will always be diversity, because unity thrives on it in order to progress.

Collaborative politics and leadership will include working with experts in different fields, who will obviously know more than politicians. With a pandemic, for instance, it would include the best scientists and medical experts working in collaboration globally and allowing them to them guide us through the science and speak directly to us. Politicians who stand and read from scripts without seeming to have any personal knowledge or conviction are not what nations need in a crisis. Instead, there should be the collective view of all nations. For instance, would closing the UK borders early on have kept the workforce intact, the children in school, wages coming in and food on the table? Would that not have been better for the people than the hardships of lockdown? That is exactly what happened in Vietnam and New Zealand, which have suffered far fewer Covid deaths.

It is time to see off climate change, racism, inequality and world poverty. To say a united world would be a safer world is an understatement. The climate threat and its deadly offshoot Covid-19 would be no match for a united, vigilant global community. Only our combined invention and ingenuity can ensure the future health of the planet but, more pertinently, to ensure that we *have* a future.

Teilhard de Chardin, almost a century ago, was convinced that: 'The age of nations is past'. Richard Horton, editor-in-chief of *The Lancet*, is also convinced that 'sovereignty is dead'. In his important book, *The Covid-19 Catastrophe*, he says much to affirm this view:

Covid-19 is a crisis about life, not health. People are ends, not means. We have edged closer together. We have rediscovered the idea of community. Our world is organised and ordered by separation and partition – countries, languages, faiths and ideologies. We must end our estrangement. My health depends on your health. Your health depends on my health. Our liberties depend on our wellbeing. We must answer the question: what do we owe each other? We need to discover our global identity. We are social beings, political beings – and mutual beings too ... Covid-19 is not an event. Instead,

it has defined the beginning of a new epoch. It took a
virus to connect us in life and in death. We understand
now, I think, our extraordinary interdependence and
unity as a species ... We surely have to use this occasion
to resist and to challenge the past mood for estrangement
and prejudice. We have to use this time for solidarity, for
mutual respect and for mutual concern ... We cannot
escape one another ... The politics and priorities of your
country are a legitimate interest of mine. Sovereignty
is dead.

33

The Unnoticed Revolution

On the whole, I think it's fair to say that human history is a record of the ways human nature has been sold short. The highest possibilities of human nature have practically always been underestimated.

Abraham H. Maslow, *Motivation and Personality*

The twentieth century saw the very basest and most extreme manifestations of what humans are capable of. Yet it's possible that the century also heralded what was to be an unnoticed yet seismic change in the history of human existence. Out of the ashes of war, terror and the depravity of the Holocaust, a tiny flame found enough oxygen to ignite a fire that would spread and enlighten great minds of the same age. Novel aspects of ordinary human beings surfaced, which in the past had been more or less ignored by science. Yet the unfolding evolution of thought, in the midst of the turmoil of the age, uncovered higher aspects of human nature. A quiet evolution was unfolding. Having reached the lowest ebb in our existence, it was to inspire and nurture more positive thinking about the higher possibilities in human nature that were previously neglected.

I have chosen three outstanding contributors to this who, alongside many more, have made a huge impact in uncovering the goodness of humanity. Teilhard de Chardin's revolutionary conviction did not come just from his paleontology, tracing the evolution of human life, but his active service in World War One as a stretcher-bearer for a Muslim regiment on the frontline. In a profound piece of writing entitled *Nostalgia for the Front*, he wrote of his experiences in that intense environment. He knew it would be difficult to communicate the experience to anyone who wasn't there. (So near impossible for me!) Yet it strikes a deep chord, incomparable to anything except the experience of anyone who, in a life-threatening situation, sees life through different eyes.

What Teilhard observed in close proximity over three years was that those engaged on the frontline, familiar with untold danger, experienced a different level of existence. The man at the front acts on behalf of his nation, but it becomes more than that. He is offering his life, knowing he may have to sacrifice it, but is willing to do so unthinkingly, not just for his own nation but for all nations. There is something compelling him that is greater than his fears and his own concerns. He is offering himself on behalf of *all* humanity. He exists on a higher plane, making his own personal contribution for the future of the world. He knows this, is certain of it and finds it exhilarating. This offer of himself affirms meaning and purpose in his existence, exposing a latent part of himself that was previously unknown to him.

Teilhard's own experience was of freedom – a release from the misguided concern for self and one's own narrow personality, to go into the trenches. His nostalgia for this intense experience must have played a huge part in his life's work and his efforts to reveal what, to him, was the awesomeness of human life.

Viktor E. Frankl, a professor of psychiatry and neurology, was, like Teilhard, able to observe humanity very closely in extreme circumstances – as a prisoner at Auschwitz. His family were sent to the gas chambers but he avoided their fate, having been deemed fit for work. The writer of the preface to his book *Man's Search for Meaning* poses a question: 'How could he – every possession lost, every value destroyed, suffering from hunger, cold and brutality, hourly expecting extermination – how could he find life worth preserving?'

What Frankl observed over three years was how humans coped in the most dehumanising of circumstances. Some lost the will to live – and there were many suicides. But others discovered that, while everything could be taken from them, one last remnant of human freedom remained intact. The ability to choose one's *attitude* and to make a decision to bear the sufferings, to be self-determining and not give up on life – this was something that remained untouched by the daily brutality of camp life.

Something more was needed beyond self-preservation: a meaning, a reason to live *for* something that would benefit from the prisoner staying alive. A child, a wife, an unfinished manuscript – a purpose that helped to endure the suffering. One of Viktor's favourite quotes was Nietzsche's: 'He who has a why to live for can bear almost any how.'

As a mind doctor, having seen and experienced this himself, he devoted his life to guiding his patients towards what he called 'logo (meaning) therapy'. All his research and

many books and papers are centred on self-actualisation and
the universal human need for meaning:

> I bear witness to the unexpected extent to which man is
> capable of defying and braving even the worst conditions
> conceivable ... Man is ultimately self-determining ...
> Man does not simply exist but always decides what his
> existence will be and what he will become in the next
> moment ... Human beings are capable of changing the
> world for the better and of changing themselves for the
> better if needed.

Another great mind I've been heavily influenced by, also
mentioned before, is Abraham H. Maslow, the famous
American professor of psychology whose research into
what he called the 'the unnoticed revolution' will remain
forever. It began with his own emotional reaction to the
Second World War. He found himself wanting to try
to understand the psychological causes of hatred and
prejudice that led to war. What was it was that had made
Hitler and Stalin such monsters? He instinctively felt that
human beings were capable of something grander and
decided to dedicate his life as a psychologist to scientifically
researching what he believed to be the inner depths and
higher nature of humanity, previously bypassed by science
and left to philosophers and theologians. His use of the
term revolution denotes radical new ways of thinking about
our inner life and personal nature, just like Frankl who had
inspired him.

The crucial element of all his research was *how it could
affect the future of society.* Volumes have been written on his
research, but the short answer was that psychologically healthy

people *knew themselves*. They were naturally self-determining. Knowing their own minds, able to make their own decisions and choices, they had learned how to be independent from outside pressures or influences. Knowing themselves freed them from being over-anxious or unsure, and meant they were less vulnerable to psychological disorders. Maslow referred to this type of person as 'self-actualised'; I prefer the words 'fully human'. The opposite of this is people who, indoctrinated by outside influences, remain ignorant of their own hidden depth and potential which, if suppressed, can cause mental instability. In severe cases, this could lead to egoism, cruelty and all we think of as bad.

Maslow was convinced that no human being is intrinsically bad. He once said, 'people are all decent underneath'; he had an amazingly contagious belief in human goodness and potential and a conviction that self-actualisation, or becoming fully human, unfettered by outside influences, is not beyond anyone's reach, but a matter of choice. We can choose to tap into unknown resources, we learn how to be ourselves and make our own choices. He describes this in blissfully simple terms: 'We are our own project, we *make* ourselves, and our project is to become fully human.' Or he describes it as self-therapy, how to help ourselves to be mentally healthy: 'Most human beings have within their own power greater possibilities than they have realised for curing themselves of a multitude of maladjustments that are common in our society ... the ultimate disease of our time is valuelessness; this state is more crucially dangerous than ever before in history' yet 'something can be done about it by humanity's own rational efforts ... the state of valuelessness ... rootlessness, emptiness, hopelessness, the lack of something to believe in and be devoted to' like 'peace, serenity, happiness … profundities that humanity has been avoiding by its busy-ness with the superficial.'

Maslow's work was rooted in his original concept that humanity was destined for something infinitely grander than war and prejudice. His certainty and enthusiasm are contagious:

> Self-actualising people have a deep identification, sympathy and affection for human beings in general. They feel a kinship and connection, as if all people were members of a single family – fully human, these people have a genuine desire to help the human race … There is now, emerging over the horizon, a new conception of human sickness and of human health that I find so thrilling and so full of wonderful possibilities … If education could awaken self-belief in children it could lead to a flowering of a new kind of civilisation.

What a vision that is, and how comforting it is to hear words of encouragement and hope from three of the greatest minds of the last century, who each saw that within the turmoil of their own time, there is a bright light within humanity that can never be extinguished.

34

The Role of Suffering

The world, seen by our experience at our level, is an immense groping, an immense search, an immense attack; its progress can take place after many failures and many wounds. Sufferers, of whatever species, are the expression of this stern but noble condition. They are not useless and dwarfed. They are simply paying for the forward march and triumph of all. They are casualties, fallen on the field of honour.

Teilhard de Chardin, *The Significance and Positive Value of Suffering*

This thought-provoking extract is from a short essay Teilhard wrote in 1933. It started out as something he wrote for his sister when she was suffering from illness, and it was later included in the book *Human Energy*. It needs to be read a few times, but it is a beautiful analogy and I have come to see that his convictions ring true.

Almost a century after it was written, I discovered an astonishing affirmation of his concept that proves, once again, that to know about humans, one need look no further than humans. Here we are, having been gifted life, on a most beautiful planet with all the resources that nurture and enrich our efforts. We are charged with making something of ourselves, which is perhaps the underlying meaning and purpose of our existence. So why do we have to suffer? Because to get to be where we want to be costs. It's a journey of groping, searching and attacking all that's wrong; it's trial and error, pain and suffering. And that is the cost involved in learning how we can flourish, build the Earth and arrive at the peace and harmony that we all long for.

Teilhard said: 'Something is afoot in the universe, a result is working out which can best be compared to a gestation and a birth.' The Earth and humanity have a mission to accomplish, a responsibility to bring about this birth in which we will triumph – and birth is, as ever, the simplest and truest analogy for suffering. After the pain of labour and the harrowing birth process, there's untold joy as the world is gifted new life and the pain soon forgotten. The cost of peace and fulfilment is no different to the cost of anything else that is worthwhile. The athlete might win the medal, but at what cost? Hours, years even, of tedious training and sacrifice, driven by the hope of eventually winning the prize. So it is with humanity. But while the athlete has his eye on the prize, he knows the cost and is willing to pay it. With humans there can be a kind of spiritual blindness that stops us from seeing the bigger picture from the inside of things. Suffering then seems cruel and pointless. The hip-hop artist Nas is among many to suggest that 'Life's a bitch and then you die.' It's an attitude that underlines the problem.

When a bigger picture emerges, the tedium and mediocrity of the daily grind give way to a renewed hope for the future.

A *desire* to be involved, a new-found zest for life, a passion for the human venture – something that might even be worth suffering or dying for! This is not naive optimism – as I've been at pains to show, this latent sense of the human mission can, whatever the cost, burst forth in moments: people are prepared to suffer, to be imprisoned or lose their lives for a cause greater than themselves. The elimination of corrupt regimes, the treatment of disease and the reversal of the damage done by climate change: everything comes at a cost, but we have seen how humans, when faced with what seem like insurmountable obstacles, have the resources both to endure and overcome suffering.

Teilhard also speaks of the transformative powers of suffering; out of tragedy, he says, something very positive can happen. One particular instance was highlighted a few years ago in a moving television drama written by my favourite screenwriter, Jimmy McGovern. He writes heart-wrenching, powerful, insightful stuff and this one, *Anthony*, told the shocking true story of the eighteen-year-old student Anthony Walker, who was brutally murdered in a vicious attack for no other reason than his colour. Anthony had wanted to go to America and become a civil rights lawyer, and Jimmy's story movingly imagines the amazing life he could have led. Fifteen years on, Anthony's mother describes a fierce pain that never leaves her. Yet her love, and that of the family for Anthony, has been formidably expressed in the form of the Anthony Walker Foundation, which aims to tackle racism and support those who experience hate crime. Out of this has come a whole network of activity, with schools and local councils giving help and support. Anthony's dream of wanting to give his life to civil rights is being enacted daily by the foundation. It is one example among countless others, which happen every day, everywhere, that show how humans have the ability to transform badness into goodness.

For me, one of Teilhard's greatest contributions is his theory that there is a positive value of suffering in those who are ill. This sounds like a contradiction and at first is impossible to comprehend. He means that the sick person has a special function to perform, in which no one can replace them: their task is cooperating in the transformation of human suffering. The sick are bearing a huge part of the pain of the world and the cost of our achievement. They are, in a sense, cut free of superficiality and more intensely aware of a truer reality. Sharing the struggle, they are connected in empathy. Their suffering is joined to the whole; united in spirit, they share in the cost of the whole human effort.

Concepts like these can only be borne out by reality, and, while I have struggled with some of the above over the years, in 2012 I came across an astonishing affirmation of what Teilhard meant. I read a powerful book entitled *When I Die: Lessons from the Death Zone* by Philip Gould – it is a quote from him that we started with on page 3. In it, he charts his own struggle with an aggressive, incurable cancer, from his diagnosis right up to the time of his death. It contains not just a record of his brave battle with the illness, but his deep insights into human existence while facing certain death. In the penultimate chapter, 'The Death Zone', he seems to have grasped, in a few short weeks, so much of life and its ultimate meaning. It is a book I would hope to have in my possession if ever I found myself in the same circumstances. Below are two short extracts:

I understand now what it's like to have pain. And I have found myself wanting to say to the world, I feel your

pain and understand the pain you are feeling. I want to
send an empathetic message to everyone.

After major surgery:

Then I felt the ventilating tube in my throat, vast
and obtrusive. I started to cough, feeling spasms of
unbearable pain in my throat where the ventilator met
my wound. The more I coughed the worse the pain,
and then it became intolerable, just beyond description.
My heart rate shot up and the pain, the panic and the
sense of suffocation combined to produce a moment of
complete blackness. I knew this was the biggest test of
my life, one that I was not certain I could pass.

I did not feel alone, though. The pain somehow
connected to the suffering of others in the world. At this
crucial moment I felt not isolation but empathy, some
kind of recognition of the power of the human spirit.

What I had not grasped from Teilhard is there in those words.
The most profound part of these extracts is that everything is
connected to the word 'world'. 'I want to share this with the
world ... I feel the pain of the world ... I am connected to
suffering of others in the world...'

The suffering, dying man *knows* he is not alone; he is
unquestionably connected to the rest of suffering humanity.
And beyond his pain in the present moment, he is happy to
know that this is so.

35

Community: The Hidden Dynamic

We hold the Earth's future in our hands and we can only progress by uniting.

Teilhard de Chardin

I think what I've been banging on about all through this book is that what we call 'common sense', in its true meaning (that between us all, there is a universally shared 'sense' of things), telling us that a strong, unified, global community is the only possible way forward. Without that, how could it be possible to achieve the harmony and peace that we all long for? This is not how things are meant to be. So finding a way to advance ourselves and our planet, in order to achieve what is surely the greatest challenge ahead of us.

I'm not talking about the Marxist ideal of everyone being lumped together, which has ended up with the same old crippling dictatorships. I mean a much more contemporary vision of interdependence and cooperation, which does not deny nations or individuals their personal identity but becomes a fusion of shared values and shared ingenuity, with all nations focused on three commonly held objectives: to value and care for our planet, in order to advance human flourishing.

We are becoming derailed because we have lost sight of those crucial objectives. Life on Earth is about people sharing their combined efforts in order to create a structure where *everyone* contributes to overcoming obstacles such as disease and climate change. What should be a shared responsibility has been wrested from the majority by a minority who, with a few exceptions, have failed spectacularly. A small percentage of people are running everything, rather badly, while the rest of us are being left out of the game.

Can we really stand by, inertly accepting what has become a very serious situation? Fascism is once more lurking in the wings via its new name, populism. Yet, just like the last time, we are in denial – as Albert Camus's novel *The Plague* prophesied. Let's not be caught off our guard once again. A united population would have the power to eradicate extreme right or left-wing ideologies and other horrors, such as people ripping down rainforests, imprisoning humans in secret concentration camps and rearing animals in unimaginably cruel conditions. Think for a moment of a united world support system, in which there are no refugees, no homelessness, no poverty and – if we want to think really big – no disease. Does that not sound like common sense? We are underestimating ourselves and the breath-taking reality of what we could achieve.

The future construction of the Earth cannot belong to a minority, but to all of us: as Teilhard says, '*we can only progress by uniting*'. This is what *has* to shape our politics. Teilhard quoted from an article that appeared in the *New Yorker* back in 1945, after the shockwaves of the Second

World War: 'Political plans for the new world, as shaped by statesmen, are not fantastic enough. The only conceivable way to catch up with atomic energy is with political energy directed towards a universal structure.' How insightful was that? Yet seventy-five years later, we still don't have a plan for a new world that is *anywhere near* fantastic enough. Science has revealed the amazing universal structure that provides human support systems, but we are threatened by the effects of not cooperating with what nature provided.

Doubts come from our innate pessimism and scepticism: how can we change things when we contemplate the sheer size of the world's population? But it only needs a small number of people to subscribe to a vision and it would soon become so contagious that it could start a common-sense revolution, a radical change of ideas that steers things in a new direction. Maslow claims that only 8 per cent of the population would need to reach a higher level of personal self-development for this to quickly spread to others. Energised people energise other people, which is *precisely* why each of us matters and what these pages have been at pains to point out. The size of the population has not deterred past revolutions: think of the great religions and other movements started by small groups that have become worldwide communities – and even without the aid of technology.

Hope has always been a distinguishing feature of humanity. The grave threats the world faces today have brought forth a new generation who, while younger in years, are more adult in attitude. They seem to have a greater cosmic sense that has alerted them to the dangers the planet is facing. They share a youthful hope and a passion that *wants* to change the world. Again, what begins as a small, united community can grow, and it is already happening. The Black Lives Matter movement has shown that if enough people around the world call time on racism, injustice and oppression, it will eventually disappear. Young people are turning out in their thousands to join forces and demand change – from Hong Kong to Thailand, Belarus to Myanmar and Russia. Many of them are willing to lose their lives or be imprisoned, while their leaders are hunted down and even poisoned. The deeper human instinct cannot be crushed – and how much we owe those who have shown that.

Figures such as Martin Luther King Jr, Nelson Mandela and many more, without thinking of themselves, have given their all in an attempt to make the world a fairer place. We are now beginning to see what happens when a groundswell of people discover the power of unity; the resulting energy can – and will – influence decisions about the future of life on Earth.

It's not rocket science, though that is a good phrase to describe something that is so glaringly obvious. A world community, differentiated but working as a whole. As we said before, *none of us could ever possibly be as smart as all of us.* The toppling of the statue of Saddam Hussein in Baghdad shortly after the invasion of Iraq in 2003 was symptomatic of a revolt against oppression. It is against nature if the majority of humans are not able to have a say in how they live their lives.

We must hope that this age of dictators, oppressive regimes and exclusive hierarchies will pass. Perhaps in the wake of Covid-19 and the threat of climate change, a younger generation with a common-sense vision for the future will become enlightened educators, because education is key. All that is wrong in the world can be summed up in one word: ignorance. As Confucius pointed out: 'Real knowledge is to know the extent of one's ignorance.' Ignorance of the valuelessness that cripples life, instead of the shared values in which a global community can unite, progress and thrive. If this could be cynically called 'utopian dreaming', I'll take it.

The dream of becoming a global community has, though, moved on apace and is being led by science and medicine. Even before Covid, the international Lancet Commission examined how it could be possible to achieve what they called a 'grand convergence' of universal healthcare, headed by the World Health Organisation, as soon as 2035. As I've already discussed, the *Lancet* editor Richard Horton's book reflects this vision very powerfully. Now, though, another optimistic book has also been published. While Covid may have taken its toll on hope, *How to Spend a Trillion Dollars: Saving the World and Solving the Biggest Mysteries in Science* by Rowan Hooper is brimming with exciting possibilities for a future in which the health and safety of the whole population becomes their responsibility.

Below is an extract:

A trillion dollars – that's one thousand billion dollars – is at once an absurdly huge amount of money, and not that much in the scheme of things. It is, give or take, 1 per cent of world GDP. It's what the US spends every year and a half on the military ... Two of the world's biggest companies, Microsoft and Amazon, are each worth more than \$1tn ... The world's richest 1 per cent together own a staggering \$162tn. That's 45 per cent of all global wealth ... Just imagine what you could do with it ... If only we could divert some of it, scrape a bit here and there from governments and banks, or quantitatively ease one trillion dollars into existence and spend it before anyone noticed. Imagine the possibilities. Imagine what we could achieve.

Let's take just one example: health care. You could eradicate malaria – hell, you could attempt to cure all diseases. Let's say our aim is to protect humanity from the next pandemic, create a new field of human biology, transform the human experience by curing, preventing or treating all known human diseases. If it sounds like I'm getting carried away, all these ideas are projects that scientists are thinking about and even working on, but are hampered by a lack of resources. [...]

Covid-19 has changed the world, and its tragedy will be felt for years, but we need to use it to raise awareness of the threat of pandemic diseases. It gives us an inkling of the threat to the world from the climate crisis ... But let's think even bigger than curing all infectious diseases ... Thousands of scientists and doctors are striving to treat and cure the world's biggest killers: cancer, cardiovascular disease and neurological disease. With an injection of cash, we could boost their chances, and see if we could transform the entire human experience by removing all illness.

Quite a statement, from quite a book. With the right amount of global investment, science and medicine are poised, in time, to eradicate *all illness*. Logically, it is – guess what – as always – common sense. The combining of human ingenuity with globally shared funding *has* to be the only way forward, as that human dynamic needs to come out of hiding to ensure a healthy, united humanity and a fully functioning planet with a certain future. *We hold the Earth's future in our hands...*

36

Love: The Fundamental Impulse of Life

Love has always been carefully eliminated from any realist and positivist concepts of the world but, sooner or later, we shall have to accept that it is the fundamental impulse of life or, if you prefer, the one natural medium in which the rising course of evolution can proceed... It is through love and within love that we must look for the deepening of our deepest selves in the life-giving coming together of humanity... To be ardently intent upon a common object is inevitably the beginning of love.

Teilhard de Chardin

Our duty is clear here. We must understand love; we must be able to teach it to create it, to predict it, or the world is lost to hostility and to suspicion.

Abraham H. Maslow

We all know about love, but we may not yet know *all* there is to know – it's a concept within the realm of human knowledge that somehow gets side-stepped. We can't even be blinded by science on this one, because science itself – for the most part – chooses to turn a blind eye. Look in the index of great scientific tomes and you won't find it mentioned. Love, scientists think, is best left to theologians and philosophers. According to Maslow, the empirical sciences and even psychology skirt around what he refers to as a 'no-man's land', as there are far easier subjects to specialise in. Is it not odd that science is intent on exploring everything that surrounds life, but does not want to even try to figure out what could be the fundamental impulse behind all that exists? Perhaps humanity will arrive at maturity when scientists, theologians and philosophers get around to combining their knowledge. It's possible that love could take us way beyond just the theory of everything and instead become the supreme solution.

Cynics would say 'dream on' – and who could blame them? Something is deeply wrong in the world, and our duty is that we *must know about love.* If it *is* the fundamental impulse of life, there's never been a more favourable time to know and understand it.

Maybe I'm being over-ambitious in attempting to step into 'no-man's land', since I am neither a scientist, a philosopher nor a theologian. But while I deeply respect their contributions, we are all equals when it comes to figuring out the meaning of love, since we all spend our lives grappling with it. It's very easy to say 'Love your neighbour', but it's impossible. Some neighbours, maybe, but certainly not others! Hence the old Yorkshire saying: 'There's none so queer as folk, save thee and me – and sometimes even thee.'

There are many misconceptions to be navigated before we arrive at the point of being able to love *all* our neighbours. Superficial feelings, for instance, are no measure of love – it's when these feelings are gone that real loving begins. Similarly, you can love very deeply beyond feelings and not really know until something triggers it. So much of what we feel is superficial, but at a deeper level we can be surprised by our own empathy. At this deeper level, love is not just possible but is as natural as breathing.

A good starting point is to divide love between that which we know and are familiar with, and that which we sense but don't truly know. We are certain of the deep love of friends, lovers, partners and families, and the joy of sexual love, which, in Teilhard's words, is 'now liberated from the duties of reproduction'. The love we all know, which can be very deep and enduring, does not end upon the death of a loved one. Then there are other passionate loves, like music, art, animals and nature. Strangely, the word love inserts itself into just about everything, from pop songs and advertising to commerce; you could say that we're obsessed with love. There are so many things we all truly love, and it wouldn't be a stretch of the imagination to say that we are a species of 'natural born lovers'. We all know that everyone wants to love and be loved; it's a fundamental impulse that's wired into our DNA.

While the above is all to do with known love, there is another *latent* love which is at the core of our existence and energises all the rest. It's hidden, but at certain moments we can be surprised and perplexed by it: ask the person diving in to save a stranger from drowning why they are willing to risk their own life, and they probably couldn't tell you. Yet it is the ultimate love, the pinnacle of how one human can care for another, inexplicably yet deeply. It's the same with health workers who have suddenly been faced with the Covid-19 crisis and risked their own lives in order to save others.

A far less noble experience for me occurred when our football club was first allowed a small number of supporters in for a game after seven months of empty, ghostly stadiums during the coronavirus pandemic. As soon as I caught sight of them sitting in the stands, I felt choked up with emotion, and I've heard that others had the same reaction. I've always loved our supporters – they are quite definitely the best in the world – but I'd never known quite how deeply I cared for them until they weren't there. What this experience revealed is so telling: we can take normal, everyday things for granted and not know we love or feel solidarity with them, until they are taken away. When I saw the world's very last northern white rhino on television I felt bereft, somehow diminished and sad that we had let that happen.

This unknown love is deeper than superficial feelings or sentiment. We don't have to strive for it because it's a part of what we are. The fact that it's not yet fully understood does not detract from its potency or its inevitability – and it's something we are evolving towards. Perhaps the word love, as it is so over-used, should be put aside and replaced by three words: *mutual internal affinity*. Whether or not it's recognised or unrecognised, felt or not felt, reasoned or not reasoned, it exists. We are part of Earth's awesome support system, which encompasses nature, plants, animal life and climate. There is a reciprocal empathy which cannot be contested, as it's not of our choosing, but it is in our very essence. We can ignore or suppress it, but we are coming towards a moment in history when each of us has to make that choice. Surely the grave threat of climate change, which threatens these natural support systems, will force us into recognising what unites us? It looks like the only course of action if we want to have a future.

I thought it was probably impossible to communicate this powerful unknown depth of love, which we *so* need to understand. Yet to my total amazement, everything I have laboured to put into words was recently demonstrated, very powerfully and right in front of my eyes. The three-minute film by Karim Sulayman called *I Trust You*, which is available on YouTube, absolutely affirms everything I've been saying. Karim, a young man from Chicago, is – like all of us – bewildered and confused about the state of the world, so he decided to stand, blindfolded, outside the Trump International Hotel and Tower in New York, alone and vulnerable, holding a board on which he'd written:

> Hello, my name is Karim and I am Arab-American. Like many people who are black, brown, women, LGBTQIA, Latin X, Muslim, Jewish, Immigrants and other, I am very scared. We are anxious and uneasy in our own country, and it's difficult to see what lies ahead for us. But I have hope that I am SAFE with you. Together we can build a community of caring rather than one of fear. You can trust me to care for you no matter who you are, what you look like or where you are from. Will you embrace me willingly as I embrace you? Will you shake my hand and/or hug me and/or take a photo of me and post it as a sign that I am safe here with you? I TRUST YOU.

What's fascinating about this extraordinary incident is watching the reactions of the people passing by. First they read the words, bemused. Then they think about it. And then they are compelled to go to him to shake his hand or to give him a hug. All types and ages, not knowing each other but unable *not* to respond and take that step of trust. In an instant, we are witnessing the fact that human instinct can be even more powerful than reason.

For me, that short clip represents a cameo of the present world. Problems, bewilderment, confusion and then, suddenly, we see the definitive and obvious answer. Instinctively, humans reach out to one another with an *inner solidarity* that can overcome the fears of the present age. This is not some impossible ideal that we can only aspire to; it is something natural and everyday that is within everyone's reach. Simply engaging with others, acknowledging what truly exists between us – why can't we see that this is all that's needed to change the world? Shared anxiety and a common sense of unease is what can initially unite us. Like strangers who become comrades in a war, perhaps the struggle to survive the effects of climate change will be our common objective, the beginning of 'the life-giving coming together of humanity'. This is not straining to love superficially, in the realm of everyday feelings, but recognising a different kind of grown-up love that opens up the bigger picture of how evolution can proceed. Humans with a *common objective* to build the Earth and make a better world. We must understand love. We must dare to believe in human life, in the whole human adventure, and we must dare to believe in love.

I hope that what has transpired within these pages has convinced you that every one of us matters and can make a unique contribution. Not convinced? No matter. In truth, it can't ever be *fully* communicated in a book. I hope, though, to have convinced you to find out more. To make a decision. To give time to stillness and reflection. To cultivate self-knowledge, self-belief and to take charge of how you use your precious time; mindful, perhaps, of the wise words of Shakespeare: 'I wasted time, and now doth time waste me.'

In the end, it will be obvious that every one of us matters in the glorious structure of life on Earth. There's an inner light waiting to be switched on, and you may never see what it can illuminate. There's an inner voice waiting to be heard, and you may never hear it. There's a human mission to be accomplished, a great tapestry to be completed, and one very important, very significant thread in it is you, because you really do *matter*. Believe in yourself, believe in the nobility and dignity of human life, and believe in those who struggle beside you. Don't close your eyes and leave this beautiful world without giving it your best shot.

Thank Yous

Nothing is ever achieved by one person, and 'None of us is as smart as all of us' applies absolutely to the team of people who have helped and supported me through writing this book. My husband Michael, who approved every chapter before I moved on to the next and cooked delicious suppers after long days at the computer. Karen Buchanan, my friend and editor, absolutely got what I was trying to do, and her insightful and helpful comments and suggestions were a vital contribution throughout. Thank you also to my lifelong agent and mentor Debbie Owen, without whom I would not have achieved anything – she did what she has always done and believed in this project from its conception. It was Debbie who encouraged me to work with Simon Juden on finding the right publisher. So a big thank you, Simon – you not only found me a publisher, but one with the noble name Mensch, run by the very 'mensch' publishing legend, Richard Charkin. Much gratitude to you both for also believing in this project. Finally, none of this would have been possible without my vital daily support team of Melanie Grocott, Lindsey Greensted Benech, Karen Whaley, Ben Tallowin and Henry Griffin, all of whom must know how their contribution and support has played an enormous part in making this book possible. Thank you so much, everyone.

Further Reading

For those who would like to read more Teilhard de Chardin,
a good book to start with is *The Legacy of Pierre Teilhard de
Chardin*, edited by James Salmon and John Farina (Paulist Press
2011). The next one I would recommend would be *The Future
of Man*, an up-to-date translation of some of his papers and
lectures. *The Human Phenomenon* is brilliantly translated by
Sarah Appleton-Weber and is the only accurate translation of
this work. A collection of Teilhard's writings are published as
The Heart of the Matter. The website of the American Teilhard
Association is www.teilharddechardin.org.

The Future of Man by Pierre Teilhard de Chardin
　　(Doubleday, 2004).

The Human Phenomenon by Pierre Teilhard de Chardin,
　　translated by Sarah Appleton-Weber (Sussex Academic
　　Press, 2003).

The Heart of the Matter by Pierre Teilhard de Chardin (Harcourt,
　　Williams 1978).

A selection of books for further reading:

Evil: Inside Human Violence and Cruelty by Roy F. Baumeister
　　(Holt, 2001).

The Conscious Mind: In Search of a Fundamental Theory by David
　　J. Chalmers (Oxford University Press, 1996).

Life's Solutions: Inevitable Humans in a Lonely Universe by Simon Conway Morris (Cambridge University Press, 2003).

Man's Search for Meaning by Viktor E. Frankl (Rider, 2004).

Meditations with Teilhard de Chardin by Blanche Gallagher (Bear & Company Books, 1988).

When I Die: Lessons from the Death Zone by Philip Gould (Little Brown, 2012).

Cosmosapiens: Human Evolution from the Origin of the Universe by John Hands (Duckworth Overlook, 2015).

An Interrupted Life: The Diaries of Etty Hillesum, 1941–43 by Etty Hillesum (Jonathan Cape, 1983).

How to Spend a Trillion Dollars: Saving the World and Solving the Biggest Mysteries in Science by Rowan Hooper (Profile Books, 2021).

The Covid-19 Catastrophe: What's Gone Wrong and How to Stop It Happening Again by Richard Horton (Polity, 2020).

The Search for Spirituality: Our Global Quest for a Spiritual Life by Ursula King (BlueBridge, 2011).

Mutual Aid: A Factor of Evolution by Peter Kropotkin (PM Press, 2018).

Exploding into Life by Dorothea Lynch and Eugene Richards (Aperture Books, 1986).

Motivation and Personality by Abraham H. Maslow (Pearson, 2007).

First Man In: Leading from the Front by Ant Middleton (Harper Collins, 2018).

The 5AM Club: Own Your Morning, Elevate Your Life by Robin Sharma (Thorsons, 2018).

Journey of the Universe by Brian Thomas Swimme and Mary Evelyn Tucker (Yale University Press, 2011).

Thomas Berry: Selected Writings on the Earth Community, edited and introduced by Mary Evelyn Tucker and John Grim (Orbis Books, 2014).

Acknowledgements

The author is grateful to the following for permission to quote from their works:

Really Useful Company (lyric from *The Phantom of the Opera*).

The *Guardian* (*Why can't the world's greatest minds solve the mystery of consciousness?*; *The Guardian view on the Thai cave rescue: a reason to be hopeful*; *From spreading happiness to saving the planet: the rise and rise of Pharrell*).

Howard Goodall and Huge Films (*Sgt. Pepper's Musical Revolution with Howard Goodall*).

Polity (extract from *The Covid-19 Catastrophe: What's Gone Wrong and How to Stop it Happening Again*, by Richard Horton).

Conde Nast Licensing for the EB White quote, *The New Yorker*.

Profile Books (extract from *How To Spend a Trillion Dollars: Saving The World and Solving the Biggest Mysteries in Science* by Rowan Hooper).

Every effort has been made to trace copyright holders and to obtain permission for the use of copyright material. The publisher apologises for any errors or omissions and would be grateful to be notified of any corrections that should be incorporated in future editions of this book.

A Note on the Author

Delia is Britain's best-loved and most trusted cookery writer and football club owner.

Delia has worked with food for over fifty years, writing columns and books and broadcasting culinary science from the ground up in a practical, accessible and straightforward style.

Delia has written many bestselling cookery books. Her aggregate book sales exceed 21 million, with Delia Smith's Cookery Course alone selling over six million copies. In addition titles such as How To Cheat At Cooking, How To Cook and Frugal Food which was published for charity.

She was appointed Companion of Honour in 2017 for her contribution to cooking and cookery education.

She lives with her husband in Suffolk and attends all of Norwich City's matches.

You can find more about Delia at www.deliaonline.com.